WHO'S INVESTING YOUR MONEY?

7 KEY QUESTIONS TO ASK YOUR FINANCIAL ADVISOR TO PROTECT YOURSELF FROM THE COMING FINANCIAL STORM

ADRIAN SPITTERS
FCSI®, CFP®, FMA, CEA

FAMILY WEALTH ADVISOR

WHO'S INVESTING YOUR MONEY?

7 KEY QUESTIONS TO ASK YOUR FINANCIAL ADVISOR TO PROTECT YOURSELF FROM THE COMING FINANCIAL STORM

Copyright 2019 by Adrian Spitters,
FCSI®, CFP®, FMA, CEA

ISBN: 978-1-895112-30-6

Published by
HeartBeat Productions Inc.
Box 633 Abbotsford, BC Canada V2T 6Z8
email: info@heartbeat1.com
604.852.3769

Edited and Layout by Dr. Win Wachsmann
Cover design, artwork: Dr. Carrie Wachsmann
Cover Photo: cogentmarketing / 123RF Stock Photo

Printed in USA

THIS BOOK IS DEDICATED
TO ALL THOSE
WHO HAVE WORKED HARD
TO ACCUMULATE WEALTH
AND WANT TO MANAGE IT WELL

TABLE OF CONTENTS

FOREWORD

For over 30 years, it has been my privilege to assist farmers, business owners, and affluent families who have accumulated substantial financial assets to protect their wealth, secure their retirement, and create a family legacy.

Through the ups and downs of the markets, local and global economic cycles, and increasing tax burdens, I have been exposed to the very best, and the very worst advice and practices the financial services industry has to offer. I have learned a great deal from my own unfortunate mistakes and, the mistakes of others. Through it all, I have been able to offer solid advice that saw my clients create multi-generational wealth.

This success is in large part because of the excellent team of advisors on whom I have relied on throughout my career to make recommendations to my clients.

Now that I have retired from the investment side of the financial services industry; I want to give fair and balanced recommendations on how to invest without corporate bias and regulatory restrictions. I now have the privilege of working with some of the top advisors in all areas of the financial services industry.

With my personal experience and interest, I am now specializing in Business, Farm, and Family Wealth Transition Planning.

Helping my business, farm, and affluent families grow and protect their wealth while keeping the taxman at bay, is especially gratifying.

While I am no longer offering investment advice, I want to point people I meet in the right direction.

Pull the curtain aside, so to speak. That is why I wrote this book.

As you read this book, reflect on the questions and ponder the implications of your past and present actions.

In this book, you will learn how to ask the right questions to select the best financial advisor for your situation.

Don't you want to join those whose careful planning paid big dividends?

Adrian Spitters,

FCSI®, CFP®, FMA, CEA

Family Wealth Advisor

CHAPTER 1

INTRODUCTION

How well does your financial advisor understand you and your financial goals?

Does the person or team investing your money understand how the financial markets and world's economic climate will impact your nest egg?

"The Following are **7 KEY QUESTIONS Every Financial Advisor** must be able to **ANSWER** To Protect Yourself From **The Coming Financial Storm.**"

Your financial freedom, security and peace of mind are at stake!

Very rarely will a financial advisor be able to answer YES to ALL 7 of these questions!

Some financial advisors do NOT even want you to know this information.

In fact, if you are – as I hope – very interested in making sure that your money is invested wisely, then take some time to read this book.

Get comfortable, ask not to be disturbed and **STUDY** this book – it is that important!

It will reveal vital information you **NEED** to know!

It's shocking but true.

Every day, farmers, business owners, and families who have accumulated substantial wealth engage financial advisors they should not be hiring. **Advisors** who quite often do not have the knowledge and expertise to manage their clients' wealth effectively.

But you can't know that.

You need the right kind of advisor working for you—particularly in today's challenging economy.

The truth is, you cannot take a risk on poor investment advice.

Can YOU answer the following questions candidly?

1. Have I saved enough?
2. What is the combined average annual return on all my investments this past year, over the past three, five or ten years?
3. Will these returns help me achieve my goals short term **AND** long term?
4. Am I comfortable with the risk level of my investments?
5. Can I reduce the tax payable on my investment income?
6. How much am I paying in fees and how are those fees affecting my investment returns?
7. What value am I really getting for the fees I am paying?

Like many investors, you may not have a clear picture of your financial health.

You've worked hard for your money and now you want your money to work hard for you!

Hiring the wrong advisor will put that goal in jeopardy.

As you know getting investment advice has never seemed easier. You now have access to specialty investment channels on TV, gurus of all shapes and sizes and websites blogs, podcasts, social media sites and newspapers all dishing out free **YET** inconsistent advice!

Get two investment advisors together and you may get four different opinions.

Here are some more questions:

1. Do you have several advisors who do not talk with each other about your overall investment strategy and financial goals?

2. Are you receiving conflicting and sometimes incomplete investment advice? Do you even know if it is incomplete?

3. Do you sometimes feel you are making investment decisions in a vacuum—without having all the information you need?

4. Do you sometimes feel your advisor has missed opportunities and even increased your tax liability?

I am going to help you make sure the next financial advisor you engage will be the best advisor your money can buy.

With the information I will give you, **you will be well-advised** and will make the best decision for you and your family.

In just a minute, I'm going to reveal the **7 Key Questions,** but first let me answer a couple of questions that are probably on your mind:

Who Are You And Why Are You Revealing This Information?

 My name is Adrian Spitters. I am President and *Family Wealth Advisor* at Performance Financial Consultants Ltd. and have extensive experience in *Integrated Family Wealth Planning.*

I come from a family business background having grown up on a dairy farm on Nicomen Island near Mission, BC and have immediate family and relatives operating dairy, poultry, and crop farms.

I began my career offering investment advice to my natural market: family, relatives, and friends operating dairy, poultry, and crop farms, as well as family businesses connected to the ag community.

I saw a number of families suffer because they had the wrong advisors.

My father, like many farmers, business owners, and families with substantial wealth of his generation, kept the family finances private. My brothers and I were not involved in my father's estate planning.

All I remember is my dad telling us that he wanted the farm to stay in the family, that he had arranged to make sure that happened, and that we would all be treated fairly in his will.

His will and estate plan were a complete mystery to my brothers and I until he passed away 20 plus years ago.

As co-executor of my father's estate, I know the painful truth of not having a proper farm transition plan and estate plan in place.

Our Dad had a poorly executed Will and a *non-existent* Tax and Estate Plan to transfer family wealth to the next generation. *The result:* family discord.

Despite receiving most of the assets, my brother, who inherited the farm, suffered financial distress and became insolvent.

The wealth my father had accumulated in his lifetime was lost in **ONE** generation. As a *Family Wealth Advisor*, I see this happening quite often and wouldn't wish it on anyone.

Our family's struggles opened my eyes to the needs of farmers, business owners, and families with substantial wealth.

Other families were experiencing similar challenges

with family wealth, farm, and business transitions.

Affluent families, farmers, and business owners with multiple assets to manage are often secretive and controlling. Even though they assume that their children will take over managing the family wealth, farm, or business, they do not want to let go of the day-to-day management and financial control. As a result, the patriarch *does not* effectively prepare their children to take over when the time comes.

This lack of preparing the next generation to inherit the family wealth, business, or farm caused me to rethink my role in my clients' lives.

Today, I work collaboratively with a team of accounting, legal, financial, insurance, investment, banking, and estate planning professionals to help business owners, farmers and affluent families and their trusted advisors avoid the mistakes my father made.

Without a documented plan in place, you can be more susceptible to an involuntary sale or transfer of the family business or farm and other family assets. A formal transition plan puts you in charge of a voluntary transition, giving you a greater choice about how and when you begin this important process.

As you read this book, reflect on the questions and ponder the implications of your past and present actions.

In this book, you will learn how to ask the right questions to select the best financial advisor for your situation.

Don't you want to join those whose careful planning paid big dividends?

You may be wondering:

What Is a Wealth Advisor and Why Should You Care?

Wealth Advisors offer more than just investment advice.

A *Wealth Advisor's* advice encompasses all parts of a person's personal and business life.

A person's wealth is not just what they have in their investment portfolio - it's everything they have accumulated: their home, their business or farm, investment property, etc.

To manage all these assets requires the advice of multiple professionals from accountants, lawyers, investment advisors, realtors, bankers, mortgage brokers, insurance agents, financial planners, estate planners and many more.

Most of these advisors usually work in isolation from each other. This isolation can result in conflicting and sometimes incomplete advice, leading to bad financial decisions that happen in isolation of a person's overall financial objectives and needs.

The reality is, while most people have an investment plan, an insurance plan, a tax plan, and maybe even a business or farm succession plan and/or estate plan, these plans were most likely done for them at different times by different advisors in isolation of each other.

The result is a collection of investments, insurance, business, farm, and trust structures that are fragmented and may not be tax-efficient, resulting in missed opportunities, and unnecessary expense, unforeseen tax liability, duplication of obligations and at worst, *catastrophic consequences*.

Rather than trying to make sense of the sometimes-conflicting advice from these *various* professionals, families with complex financial assets, business owners ,and farm families can benefit from *taking* a holistic approach to managing their wealth.

This approach involves using a single *Wealth Advisor* who coordinates *all* the *services/consultants* required to manage their wealth and plan for their own and/or their family's current and future needs.

Wealth Advisors start by developing a plan that will grow and protect their clients' wealth based on their clients' personal financial situation, goals, comfort level, risk tolerance, and needs.

This *plan* would encompass:

- an investment plan to manage their investments;

- a risk plan to manage the risks to their wealth and livelihood;

- a personal tax plan to manage the tax implications of managing their personal wealth;

- a family, business or farm tax plan;

- a family wealth transition plan;

- a business or farm transition plan to plan the transition or sale of their business or farm to their children or new owners when they retire in a tax-efficient manner; and

- an estate plan to transfer their assets to the next generation tax-efficiently that also meets their wishes on who gets what and how.

Once all these plans are created, the *Wealth Advisor* works with their clients' own network of professionals to implement the various components of their plan and then meets with them on a regular basis to review and monitor the progress of their plans.

These plans are revised and updated when needed. *Wealth Advisors* touch every aspect of their clients' wealth from growing, protecting, and transferring their wealth to the next generation.

Wealth Advisory Team

Most financial advisors are not *Wealth Advisors*. They do not have the knowledge or access to integrated and comprehensive wealth management services.

So how do you find a Wealth Advisor that can offer all the services mentioned above?

Good question!

Let's talk about the **7 Key Questions Every Financial Advisor MUST Be Able to Answer** To Protect Yourself from **The Coming Financial Storm**.

Now... you may be expecting a series of questions like:

"Do you have any samples of the types of portfolios you recommend?"

"Can you show me testimonials?"

"What is your track record?"

All those are good questions. Any financial advisor worth their salt will have ready responses in place.

As someone who has been there in the trenches with the best of them, let me lay on you some queries the average financial advisor **ISN'T** expecting... which will enable you to see who's ready to advise you on your money and family wealth.

So let's get to the 7 Key questions.

After going through them, you may still have some other questions like the following:

a. What type of advisor should I choose?

b. What can I expect in terms of fees?

c. What comprehensive services should my advisor be offering?

While the focus of this book is on investment advice, we'll cover those after we examine the *7 Key Questions*.

CHAPTER 2

QUESTION 1
FOR YOUR FINANCIAL ADVISOR

Are You a Fiduciary?

"A fiduciary is a person who has a duty of loyalty imposed upon them by the Canadian courts to a person entrusted to them. This relationship arises when a person is vulnerable to the other person due to their personal relationship or the broad scope of their authority given to that person by the person under their care."

"Professionals such as lawyers always have a fiduciary duty to their clients due to the personal nature of their relationship.

Corporate directors have a fiduciary duty to the companies they serve due to the scope of the authority they have over the company."[1]

When it comes to the handling of your money, it is important to work with an advisor that has a fiduciary duty to put your interests first. This is not the case with all levels of financial advisor registration.

```
                    Portfolio
                  Managers (PM)

               Investment Industry
             Regulatory Organization of
             Canada (IIROC) Dealers &
                     Advisors

           Mutual Fund Dealers & Advisors
                      (MFDA)

        Captive and Independent Insurance Company
                   & Advisor Channels

              Exempt Market Dealers (EMD)
```

[1] Fiduciary Duties and Financial Advisors - IFIC.ca *The Investment Funds Institute of Canada* https://www.ific.ca/wp-content/uploads/2013/08/Fiduciary-Duties-and-Financial-Advisors-Frequently-Asked-Questions-and-Answers-August-2011.pdf/1658/

Five levels of registration in Canada

1. Exempt Market Dealers (EMD)

Exempt Market Dealers (**EMDs**) are fully registered securities dealers who engage in the business of trading in prospectus exempt securities, or any securities to qualified exempt market clients. EMDs may focus on certain market sectors (e.g. oil and gas, real estate, minerals, technology, etc.) or may have a broad cross-sector business model. Clients of EMDs include companies, institutional investors, accredited investors (sophisticated or high net worth individuals who are eligible to trade securities in the exempt market), or eligible investors who are qualified to purchase exempt securities pursuant to an **Offering Memorandum**.[2]

Exempt Market Dealers (EMD) fees tend to be very lucrative:

> *"Companies are interested in maximizing the amount of capital they can raise, and dealers want to boost their commissions – so there are incentives for both groups to encourage investors to buy up a good number of securities."*[3]

[2] "*What Is the Exempt Securities Market? - Private Capital Markets Association of Canada*, https://www.pcmacanada.com/page/ESM.
[3] "Buyer Beware with Exempt Securities." *The Globe and Mail*, 21 Dec. 2017, www.theglobeandmail.com/globe-investor/globe-wealth/buyer-beware-with-exempt-securities/article37406342/.

There is usually limited public information on these investment offerings. The investor must rely on the EMD's research to make an informed decision when purchasing these securities. This research may be biased in favour of painting a favourable picture to sell the securities and not necessarily based on the merits of the investment being promoted.

Many of these investments are highly illiquid. Therefore, investors must be willing and able to wait a long time to liquidate them.

Due to the limited availability of research, the potential for conflict of interest, illiquidity, and potentially higher fees, these investments tend to be high to very high risk and should only represent no more than 10% of an investor's portfolio or not at all if the investor is risk-averse.

Over the years, many of my clients bought one or more of these investments, prior to becoming my client. I have yet to see them make money on these investments. In fact, many of these clients lost all the money they had invested.

In addition to losing all their money, some were also on the hook for loans they took out to make these speculative and potentially windfall investments. Furthermore, tax losses assured by the investment promoter were eventually denied by CRA.

"The main takeaway is that considerable care needs to be exercised in the selection of exempt securities, lest investors end up with a collection that does not fit their needs. This may not be such a big concern when a rising economic tide is lifting all boats. But when the cycle turns and companies begin to struggle, it could be another story."[4]

2. Captive and Independent Insurance Channels

The distinction between Insurance Advisors is somewhat muddied. Some insurance advisors work directly for the insurance companies that hired them to sell their proprietary insurance products and are known as Captive Insurance Advisors.

In contrast, independent advisors have contracts with Managing General Agents (MGAs) and can represent the products of several different insurance companies. Representing various companies gives the agent a greater choice of products to best serve their clients' needs.

Both *Captive and Independent insurance advisors (agents) may* offer investment products known as segregated funds. These funds are like mutual funds with an insurance component added.

[4] Buyer Beware with Exempt Securities." *The Globe and Mail* , 21 Dec. 2017, www.theglobeandmail.com/globe-investor/globe-wealth/buyer-beware-with-exempt-securities/article37406342/

Segregated funds may or may not be suitable for many clients as they generally have higher fees associated with them. The fees are generally higher than mutual funds fees because they are insurance contracts that offer certain guarantees of a partial or full refund of the principal after a predetermined time or on the death of the investor. These fees, also known as **Management Expense Ratios** or **(MERs)**, generally range from 2.7% to over 4%.

There are very few instances where a segregated fund would be beneficial for an investor. Many segregated funds are actually a replication of existing mutual funds with an insurance contract wrapped around them. So, for most investors, the underlying mutual fund would be a better investment because of the lower fees.

Now you can argue that segregated funds bypass probate when the fundholder dies. However, when bypassing probate, you're only saving 1.4% one time.

Investing in a segregated fund and paying up to an extra 1.5% per year to invest in the segregated fund, loses its benefit if you own it for a little over a year. You will have lost the benefit of saving the probate fee after the first year of investing in the fund.

In my opinion, there are only two reasonable times that one should invest in a segregated fund.

The *first* is when an investor needs creditor protection, and hopefully, they are not already in a financially dire situation because it won't matter, as they are not protected.

The *second* is when they want to pass a certain amount of money on to the next generation through an investment, and they do not want anyone to know about it. That might be a good time to invest in a segregated fund. However, they need to understand that they will be paying higher fees to accomplish this. There may be other, more cost-effective ways to accomplish this, such as *Family Trusts* and *Alter Ego Trusts*.

3. Mutual Fund Dealer Association of Canada (MFDA)

Mutual funds are generally sold by advisors working at MFDA regulated mutual fund dealers, brokerage firms, and at your local bank branch.

> *"The fund's management fee and operating expenses make up a fund's Management Expense Ratio or **MER**. They are paid by the fund and are expressed as an annual percentage of the total value of the fund. Mutual Fund **MERs** (fees) can range from less than 1% to more than 3%. While you don't pay these expenses directly, they affect you because they reduce the fund's returns. This can add up over time."* [5]

[5] "Mutual Fund Fees: Mutual Funds & Segregated Funds." *GetSmarterAboutMoney.ca*, www.getsmarteraboutmoney.ca/invest/investment-products/mutual-funds-segregated-funds/mutual-fund-fees/.

Mutual funds may or may not be an appropriate choice for investors with large investment portfolios as many mutual funds are over diversified and may not be actively managed. As a result of this over-diversification, many mutual funds may resemble closet indexers, i.e., they may closely resemble a market index or benchmark.

3a. Closet Indexing

Mutual fund managers and insurance-based segregated funds managers are continuously measured by investment researchers, media, and the public against market indexes. These measurements may cause managers to mirror the benchmark against which they are measured, resulting in returns before management fees that may be very close to the benchmark, but lag the benchmark after subtracting their management fee. After the management fee, these funds generally lag the market benchmark by the fee they charge.

> *"Closet indexing is a strategy used to describe funds that claim to actively purchase investments but wind up with a portfolio not much different from the benchmark. By doing so, **Portfolio Managers** achieve returns similar to an underlying benchmark, like the S&P 500, without exactly replicating the index. The motivation for closet indexing grows out of years of poor performance and the ongoing shift from active to passive management.*

Flows out of active and into passive funds have topped hundreds of millions in assets under management for multiple years. This has put pressure on fund managers who fear the passive industry will eliminate stock-picking jobs." [6]

Since many mutual funds are effectively closet index funds, why would you pay up to 3% annual **MER** fee for a mutual fund and up to 4% for a segregated fund that may mirror a market index, when you can essentially get the same results from an unmanaged Exchange Traded Fund (ETF) that has a low average **MER** fee of 0.3%? The result, mutual funds and segregated funds that appear to mirror a benchmark index could underperform the benchmark by up to 3% - 4% (the **MER**), respectively when a similar ETF would only underperform the benchmark by .3%.

4. Investment Industry Regulatory Organization of Canada (IIROC)

The Investment Industry Regulatory Organization of Canada (IIROC) regulated firms include all your bank-owned brokerage firms and independent stockbrokers. IIROC firms sell stocks, bonds, mutual funds, and Exchange Traded Funds (ETFs).

---

[6] Chen, James. "Closet Indexing." *Investopedia*, Investopedia, 21 July 2019, www.investopedia.com/terms/c/closetindexing.asp.

Fees at IIROC firms vary and can range from 1.5% to 2.75% depending upon the portfolio strategy and investments recommended.

Self-Regulatory Organizations (SROs)

The key with three of the four levels of licensing, (IIROC, MFDA & Insurance) is that they are Self-Regulatory Organizations (SROs). They are not part of a national regulatory body since Canada does not have one. They are instead regulated by individual provincial security regulatory bodies in which the organization does business.

EMDs are subject to full dealer registration and compliance requirements and are directly regulated by the provincial securities commissions.[7]

The key thing to understand here is that IIROC, MFDA & Insurance advisors may or may not be a fiduciary. This will depend on the relationship they have with their clients and the designations they have.

> *"Pursuant to Canadian common law, whether or not a financial advisor would be found to be a fiduciary to his or her client would depend on the particular facts.*

[7] *What Is the Exempt Securities Market? - Private Capital Markets Association of Canada,* https://www.pcmacanada.com/page/ESM

The existence of fiduciary duty in a given situation would depend upon the reasonable expectations of the parties based on such factors as vulnerability, trust, reliance, discretion, confidence, the complexity of the subject matter, and community or industry standards.

The sort of advisor-advisee relationship that would likely be found not to be fiduciary in nature would be one where the client simply placed orders with a discount broker who then carried out the requested transaction.

On the other hand, an advisor-advisee relationship that would likely be found to be fiduciary in nature would be one where an elderly, unsophisticated client placed his or her retirement savings in the hands of an investment advisor to invest as the advisor deemed necessary to achieve certain investment objectives for the client (e.g., to provide income through retirement)." [8]

When there is an infraction with an advisor in a non-fiduciary relationship in one of these SRO organizations, they may be given a slap on the wrist, fine, suspension, or lose their license. They may not be held accountable to a higher fiduciary standard.

[8] "Fiduciary Duties and Financial Advisors - Ific.ca." *The Investment Funds Institute of Canada*. N.p., n.d. Web. 11 Jul. 2019 https://www.ific.ca/wp-content/uploads/2013/08/Fiduciary-Duties-and-Financial-Advisors-Frequently-Asked-Questions-and-Answers-August-2011.pdf/1658/

Many of the transparency issues have erupted and continue to erupt in these organizations, where they may not be fully compliant and transparent on their fees and the performance of the products they sell.

5. Portfolio Manager (PM)

Unlike the previous four registrations where the advisor may be a fiduciary depending on their relationship with their clients, *Portfolio Managers (PMs)* are fiduciaries by law. The *Chartered Financial Analyst (CFA)*, as well as the *Chartered Investment Manager (CIM),* make up this group.

The **CFA** is a world-wide recognized designation. **CFA's** can operate as a *Portfolio Manager* anywhere in the world, whereas the **CIM** is a Canadian only designation.

Portfolio Managers are not self-regulated. Instead, they are regulated by each individual provincial securities commission.

Portfolio Managers have a fiduciary duty to their clients as they are held to a higher standard. As fiduciaries, the provincial securities regulators require *Portfolio Managers* to have the highest level of education and experience in the investment industry.

A *Portfolio Manager* is the highest level of licensing in Canada and globally. They are registered and monitored directly by provincial securities commissions. They must also meet strict financial reporting, capital, and insurance requirements to protect their clients' investments.

> *"In Canada,* **Portfolio Managers** *have to act with care, honesty, and good faith. They must always act in the best interest of their clients. This is called a* **"Fiduciary Duty."** *All their investment decisions, therefore, must be independent and free of bias.*
>
> *Because of this requirement,* **Portfolio Managers** *receive a higher level of trust from their clients."*[9]

Due to the discretionary nature of their role, a fiduciary must always put their clients' interests **FIRST**.

Portfolio Managers must recommend investments that are suitable for their client's investment goals and risk tolerance. They are obligated to give their clients full fee and investment performance transparency.

Portfolio Managers do not charge commissions. Instead, they charge a flat fee that is reduced based on the size of the client's portfolio. The larger the portfolio, the lower the fee. Fees for non-registered accounts are also tax-deductible.

[9] "What Is A Portfolio Manager? - Pmac." Portfolio Management Association of Canada. N.p., n.d. Web. 12 Jul. 2019 https://pmac.org/nav-investor-info/selection-checklist/.

CHAPTER 3

QUESTION 2
FOR YOUR FINANCIAL ADVISOR

Do you have full, discretionary trading authority?

Portfolio Managers, are discretionary, meaning they can make investment decisions on their client's behalf fast and efficiently since they do not need to call their clients every time, they make an investment decision.

*"They do this by creating an individual written agreement or **Investment Policy Statement (IPS)** with their clients to establish and set out how their*

clients will work with them, including ongoing communication, types of investments, reporting, fees, risks and other issues related to their client's own circumstances.[10]

Having discretionary trading authority is important, especially during market volatility, where the advisor needs to adjust a client's portfolio to protect them or to take advantage of a unique opportunity that presents itself.

In Canada, in order for an advisor in an SRO-regulated organization discussed in Question 1, to make a trade-in your portfolio, they must call you first to discuss the trade and get your agreement to make the trade. In many cases, you must sign off on the transaction before the transaction can be made in your portfolio.

If you are not one of the top 10 people on the advisor's list to get that phone call, your transaction is probably not done in a timely manner. For example, in a declining market, if the advisor recommends selling specific securities in their clients' portfolios to avoid major losses, they start calling their top clients first. Each client is treated individually and in order of importance to the advisor or their availability to be reached.

---

[10] "What Is A Portfolio Manager? - Pmac." Portfolio Management Association of Canada. N.p., n.d. Web. 12 Jul. 2019 https://pmac.org/nav-investor-info/selection-checklist/

Given that many successful advisors can have over 1,000 clients, it can take weeks before the advisor can reach, meet, and suggest transactions for all their clients. The reverse also happens in a recovering market. When unique investment opportunities arise, the advisor must contact all their clients to make the transaction. Guess who gets called first and last?

This can't happen with a ***Portfolio Manager (PM)***. They are subject to what is called the "***Fair Dealing Standard***." Under the fair dealing standard, ***Portfolio Managers*** must make the same changes to all their client's portfolios at the same time and for the exact same price. All clients must be treated equally.

> *"Under the Fair Dealing Standard **Portfolio Managers** must deal fairly and objectively with all clients when providing investment analysis, making investment recommendations, taking investment action, or engaging in other professional activities."*[11]

---

[11] *"Standard III(B) Fair Dealing." CFA Institute*https://www.cfainstitute.org/en/ethics/codes/std-of-practice-guidance/stds-of-practice-III-B

In order to comply with the fair dealing standard, a *Portfolio Manager* must have discretionary authority to make investment trades in all their clients' portfolios at the same time without having to get their clients to sign off on the transaction first.

This ability allows the *Portfolio Manager* to maneuver efficiently and promptly to protect their client's portfolios in a *Down Market* and to take advantage of investment opportunities in *Up Markets*. Since *Portfolio Managers* can make discretionary investment decisions on behalf of all their clients at the same time, their clients are treated equally and fairly, regardless of how much a client has invested with the *PM*. This discretionary process results in consistent portfolio returns for *ALL* clients.

Many IIROC firms employ advisors that call themselves *Portfolio Managers* and have the *Chartered Investment Manager (CIM)* designation. Many of these advisors may not have discretionary trading authority, because every time they make a trade recommendation on behalf of their client, they must get approved by a *Chartered Financial Analyst (CFA)* employed at the firm's head office, usually in Toronto. These trades can take up to a day for approval, and because each trade must be approved for each client, they are not timely.

In contrast, a ***Discretionary Portfolio Manager*** has the authority to make discretionary trades on behalf of all their clients at the same time without having to call their clients individually to make the trade. This way, all trades are done promptly, and all clients, regardless of size, are treated equally.

CHAPTER 4

QUESTION 3
FOR YOUR FINANCIAL ADVISOR

Do you offer a written investment plan outling how my money will be invested?

As you may know, investing is a trade-off between *Risk and Return*. On the one hand, lower risk investments may guarantee your money but often provide lower returns.

On the other hand, many investments offering higher returns can come with a greater level of risk. The trade-off is finding the right balance for you.

Your written investment plan (also called an *Investment Policy Statement (IPS)*) should detail the **amount of risk with which you are comfortable, along with your expected rate of return.**

Your plan should be based on the following variables:

1. your need for income;

2. where you are in life;

3. if and when you need access to cash;

4. growth expectations of your investments;

5. income tax characteristics;

6. your tolerance for market volatility (risk);

7. anticipated changes in your lifestyle; and

8. economic variables that affect your portfolio such as inflation and market volatility.

*"An investment policy statement (**IPS**) is a document drafted between a **Portfolio Manager** and a client that outlines general rules for the manager. This statement provides the general investment goals and objectives of a client and describes the strategies that the manager should employ to meet these objectives.*

*In addition to specifying the investor's goals, priorities and investment preferences, a well-conceived **IPS** establishes a systematic review process that enables the investor to stay focused* *on the long-term objectives, even as the market gyrates wildly in the short term. It should contain all current account information, current allocation, how much has been accumulated, and how much is currently being invested in various accounts."[12]*

Your assets should be invested using these guidelines and be itemized in the ***Investment Policy Statement (IPS)***. Your ***Wealth Advisor*** and/or ***Portfolio Manager*** will need to confirm with you regularly that they are following these guidelines.

Your **IPS** should illustrate the historical volatility of your proposed portfolio over a one year, three year, five year, and ten-year time frame.

The portfolio asset mix and the strategies your ***Portfolio Manager*** will use to achieve the predicted results should be clearly defined.

Look for a customized plan based on your demands and needs, not some boilerplate plan that can easily be modified to suit anyone.

[12] Kagan, Julia. "Introduction to the Investment Policy Statement (IPS)." *Investopedia* Investopedia, 6 July 2019, https://www.investopedia.com/terms/i/ips.asp.

The Optimal Portfolio

*"One assumption in investing is that a higher degree of risk means a higher potential return. Conversely, investors who take on a low degree of risk have a low potential return. According to Markowitz's theory, there is an **Optimal Portfolio** that could be designed with a perfect balance between risk and return. The **Optimal Portfolio** does not simply include securities with the highest potential returns or low-risk securities. The **Optimal Portfolio** aims to balance securities with the greatest potential returns with an acceptable degree of risk or securities with the lowest degree of risk for a given level of potential return. The points on the plot of risk versus expected returns where **Optimal Portfolios** lie are known as the **Efficient Frontier**."*[13]

The portfolio on the chart below labelled "*Current Portfolio*" is an inefficient portfolio as it is under the *Efficient Frontier* (curved line on the graph).

The curved line represents all the possible *Optimal Portfolios* for a given rate of return and a given level of risk.

---

[13] Ganti, Akhilesh. "Efficient Frontier Definition." *Investopedia*, Investopedia, 1 Apr. 2019, https://www.investopedia.com/terms/e/efficientfrontier.asp.

An ***Optimal Portfolio*** would fall on the ***Efficient Frontier***. As you can see for the same amount of risk as the current portfolio, you can move the portfolio up to the ***Efficient Frontier*** line to achieve a higher rate of return on the vertical axis labelled ***Managed Account Premium***, or for the same rate of return you can significantly reduce the risk of the current portfolio by moving the portfolio to the left on the horizontal axis labelled ***Downside Risk*** onto the ***Efficient Frontier***.

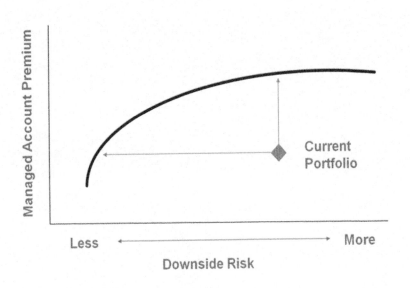

CHAPTER 5

QUESTION 4
FOR YOUR FINANCIAL ADVISOR

Do you have an asset allocation process in place to maximize your clients' portfolio returns while minmizing risk?

Source: LCM Perspectives, September 15, 1997, For illustrative purposes only.

Financial Advisors generally use two types of asset allocation strategies. These strategies are known as Tactical and Strategic.

1. Tactical Asset Allocation involves an element of market timing and moving in and out of various *Asset Classes*.

While this sometimes appears as an attractive strategy to investors, it has been shown that market timing does not work very well, is not very tax efficient, and costs investors over the longer-term.

Tell me if this story sounds familiar.

We know that over time, investments go up and down, but that is what makes investing fun, right?

Imagine that you are around a water-cooler and a few friends are talking about a great stock they recently bought, and are trying to convince you that it is a great buy.

Eventually, the pressure gets too much, and you buy it.

What happens after you buy it? The value of the stock goes up, and you're feeling upbeat and like an investing pro.

Then, not unexpectedly, the stock goes down. After a few weeks of down, you are still all right. Then after it has gone down by 50%, you feel like the markets just aren't for you. What emotion are you experiencing at this point? **FEAR!**

You may be affected by *Recency Bias*. As the value of your stock goes down, you may become concerned.

Recency Bias is, "...the tendency to think that trends and patterns we observe in the recent past will continue into the future."

The value of a stock that has dropped in value will continue to drop. "I must sell my stock to reduce my losses."

Should you sell, you will lock in your losses. Had you waited, you might have seen the trend reverse and the value of the stock move up. Now you're kicking yourself.

But in this case, your investment turns around, and it starts to go up.

Recency Bias sets in again, and you buy in order not to lose out on the projected profits.

Eventually, the stock gets back up to the same price that you paid for it. What emotion are you experiencing at this point? **HOPE!**

You may feel tempted to sell and get out without having lost anything, but then again, it is going so well that you decide to stay in for a little longer.

Now the third emotion kicks in — **GREED!** Now you put in more money into the investment. Then what happens?

What we can see from this scenario, if we look at the market as a whole, is that the high points are the ones with the most financial risk, and the low points are the places where we have the most financial opportunity.

The sheer volume of information and our emotions both hurt our ability to make the best investment decisions possible.

When we look at investing, there are certain truths that we know work.

For many retail investors, these emotions translate into action. They tend to panic sell when the markets are going down, selling great stocks with the not-so-great stocks, because they do not have the expertise to understand what to keep, so instead of selling only the bad stocks, they tend to sell everything. These sales cause the market correction to accelerate as the inexperienced retail investor panics.

"To buy when others are despondently selling and to sell when others are avidly buying requires the greatest of fortitude and pays the greatest ultimate rewards."[14]
- Sir John Templeton

[14]"John Templeton Quotes." *Quotewise.com.* N.p., n.d. Web. 01 Aug. 2019 http://www.quoteswise.com/john-templeton-quotes.html

Professional **Portfolio Managers** take advantage of these market corrections. They would have long ago decided on what stocks they want to own and at what price. If the stock they want to purchase is slightly overpriced, they wait until the uninformed investors panic, bring the price of the stock down to where it is attractive for them to purchase the stock.

In a market correction, the target company's outlook will, in all probability, not have changed substantially. Only the emotional selling perspective in the market will have taken a hit. **Portfolio Managers** see market corrections as a buying opportunity, not a reason to panic.

Many Financial Advisors that favour market timing offer misleading facts such as:

"If you miss the 10 best days of the stock market over 30 years, you would actually have negative returns." This is true. However, it is a one-sided argument, and fails to consider "what if I miss the 10 worst days?" One study shows missing the 10 worst days more than triples a buy and hold strategy. However, both arguments are flawed and misleading. For example, if you started investing in 1963, you would find that at the end of 1983 you had less money than you started with 20 years later.

The point being is you need a long-term investment plan in place with a discipline strategy to make the outcome for your portfolio meet your own specific goals - and you should avoid these types of "what ifs." [15]

Portfolio Managers understand that no one can time the market with such precision as to miss the 10 worst days of the market or to only invest in the 10 best days in the market. Instead of timing the markets, **Portfolio Managers** rely on a strategy known as **Strategic Asset Allocation**.

2. Strategic Asset Allocation is the philosophy and approach that involves setting up a target asset mix of various **Asset Classes** that provide investors with the maximum rate of return given their risk level.

The portfolio is rebalanced periodically back to its original allocation when it deviates from the original portfolio allocation due to differing returns from the various assets in the portfolio.

---

[15] "Portfolio Asset Allocation Investing Strategies Santa Barbara & Los Angeles Asset Manager I How to Invest, How to Protect Your Portfolio from Loss Risks & Free Investing Advice Stocks, Bonds, Alternative Assets." *Montecito Capital Management I Building Brighter Futures*, https://www.mcapitalmgt.com/portfolio.html

"The target allocations depend on several factors, such as the investor's risk tolerance, time horizon, and investment objectives, and may change over time as these parameters change.

***Strategic Asset Allocation** is compatible with a buy-and-hold strategy, as opposed to tactical asset allocation that is more suited to an active trading approach. Strategic and tactical asset allocation styles are based on **Modern Portfolio Theory**, which emphasizes diversification to reduce risk and improve portfolio returns."*[16]

Research has shown that how a portfolio is constructed is responsible for over 90% of a portfolio's return over time. Security selection and market timing are minimal contributors to a portfolio's overall return.

---

[16] "Strategic Asset Allocation - *Investopedia*." N.p., n.d. Web. 01 Aug. 2019 https://www.investopedia.com/terms/s/strategicassetallocation.asp.

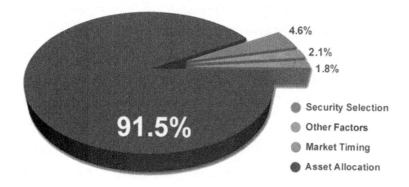

4.6%
2.1%
1.8%

● Security Selection
● Other Factors
● Market Timing
● Asset Allocation

91.5%

Source: Determinants of Portfolio Performance, Gary P. Brinson | L. Randolph Hood | Gilbert L. Beebowe

This is a longer-term, more disciplined, and tax-efficient process and the approach I recommend.

Your financial advisor should focus on:

- A portfolio's after-tax returns. What's the point of getting high returns, only to have taxes erode your gains?
- Total returns over time rather than shooting out the lights one year, only to lose money the next year.
- What they can control, such as costs, taxes, and a disciplined investment process instead of the market which they cannot control.

CHAPTER 6

QUESTION 5
FOR YOUR FINANCIAL ADVISOR

How do you invest your clients' money?

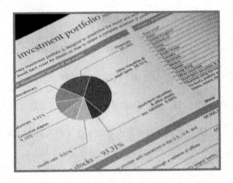

Do you make the investment decisions yourself, or do you delegate the investment decisions to a team of professional *Private Money Managers*?

When it comes to investing your money, your investment advisor has three choices they can make:

1. Your advisor can choose to buy stocks and bonds (generally done through a stock broker);

2. Your advisor can decide to invest in mutual funds which provide professional money management; or

3. Your advisor can employ dedicated, professional, **Private Money Managers.**

1. Stocks and Bonds

If your advisor recommends stocks and bonds, he/she will either:

A. act as principal recommending stocks/bonds from their in-house brokerage account; or

B. act as agent by going out to an exchange and purchasing the stocks/bonds on your behalf.

Trading as Principal

"Principal trading occurs when a brokerage buys securities in the secondary market, holds these securities for a period of time, and then sells them. The purpose behind principal trading is for firms (also referred to as dealers) to create profits for their own portfolios through price appreciation.

So, when an investor buys and sells stock through a brokerage firm that acts as the principal to trade, the firm will use its own inventory on hand to fill the order for the client. With this method, brokerage firms earn extra income (over and above the commissions charged) by making money from the bid-ask spread as well.

For instance, if you were looking to buy 100 shares of ABC at $10, the principal firm would first check their own inventory to see whether the shares are available to sell to you. If they are available, the firm would sell the shares to you and then report the transaction to the necessary exchange."[17]

There is potential for abuses to occur when a brokerage firm purchases securities for their own portfolios at wholesale or initial price offerings and then sells the same security to their clients at current retail or appreciated prices. If the brokerage firm has a significant client base across the country, they may have influence in the marketplace and can move the value of the stock prices up or down. These brokerage firms frequently offer free research on specific stocks through the media. This is where the abuse could come into play.

[17] "Principal Trading and Agency Trading - *Yahoo Finance.*" N.p., n.d. Web. 23 Jul. 2019 https://finance.yahoo.com/news/principal-trading-agency-trading-170000752.html.

An example of potential abuse would be when a brokerage firm's research department intentionally identifies a security as a great investment opportunity for their own inventory and then holds it for a while before issuing a buy recommendation to the marketplace and their clients. As they sell the stock out of inventory as principal, the brokerage firm not only makes money on the commissions generated from selling the stock, they also make money on the rise in the stock's value as they promote the stock to their clients.

In this scenario, the brokerage firm is not acting in their client's best interest, as they are profiting from recommending the stock they hold in their own inventory.

They are acting in their own self-interest and, therefore, NOT in their clients' best interest as a fiduciary.

IPO's Legalized Looting

"A majority of IPO's have been launched in the form of 'legalized looting' by company promoters and their investment bankers.

I have come to believe how Benjamin Graham defined IPOs in The Intelligent Investor. He said that intelligent investors should conclude that IPO does not stand only for 'initial public offering.'

More accurately, it is a shorthand for…

- **It's Probably Overpriced; or**
- **Imaginary Profits Only; or even**
- **Insiders' Private Opportunity.**"[18]

Another potential for abuse occurs when an investment dealer sells an **IPO** to their investment clients. Investment broker-dealers may also act as underwriters. In other words, they will act to underwrite the issue of new securities of a new company or underwrite new issues of a company wishing to raise more money. This is usually done at a time when the markets are at all-time highs, giving the company the best opportunity to raise the most money at a time when investors are most receptive to purchasing new stock.

Many dealers acting as underwriters would underwrite the new securities as a bought deal, meaning that they will own the security. They would set a price for the security by sending out feelers into the marketplace to determine the interest in the new security. Based on that, they would set the price - usually for much more than the stock is worth.

---

[18] "3 Reasons IPOs Are Almost Always Bad Investments | *Safal Niveshak*". N.p., n.d. Web. 23 Jul. 2019 https://www.safalniveshak.com/3-reasons-ipos-are-bad-investments/.

The underwriter would charge the company raising the money up to 7%[19] of the money raised as commission for underwriting the new stock issue. As a bought deal, the underwriter owns the stock. Since the stock by nature is already overvalued, the underwriter does not want to hold onto the stock for very long, they would send allotments to each of their branch brokerage-dealer offices based on the volume of business they do for the firm. Then the branch manager issues an allotment to each of the brokers in the branch with marching orders to sell the securities to investors.

Finding investors to invest can be a challenge. Since it is easier to sell stocks to their existing clients, many stockbrokers will go to their own clients to sell the new *IPO*. They would identify a stock in their client's portfolio that they can convince their client to liquidate to raise the money to purchase the new *IPO*. By doing this, not only will the brokerage firm earn a commission for selling the *IPO*, but they would also earn a commission from selling the stock to raise the money to purchase the *IPO*.

In this scenario, the brokerage firm is *acting in their own self-interest and NOT as a fiduciary. They are NOT acting in their clients' best interest.*

---

[19] PricewaterhouseCoopers. "Considering an IPO to Fuel Your Company's Future?" *PwC,* www.pwc.com/us/en/services/deals/library/cost-of-an-ipo.html

At the height of the dot-com bubble, I remember my neighbour across the street, who worked as an assistant to one of the top stockbrokers at a national brokerage firm in Vancouver, brag about how they were calling their clients to sell perfectly good stocks to raise money to purchase Nortel, JDS Uniphase, Research In Motion, 360networks, Worldcom and other highly questionable stocks.

The stocks they were selling were bank and resource stocks that were underperforming because of the selling pressure from brokerage firms raising money to purchase dot-com stocks.

This was definitely an example of self-serving actions by the brokerage firm as these bank and resource stocks did exceptionally well once the dot-com bubble burst in 2000. They were up up significantly a year later, while dot-com stocks lost as much as 50% or more, with many going bankrupt.

I resisted liquidating bank and resource stocks to purchase dot-com stocks to my clients' dismay, only to be praised by my clients after the dot-com bubble burst as they made money while the markets crashed.

Investors Salutatory Rights

Many investors may feel pressured to purchase an **IPO** recommeded by their broker and have regrets in not making an informed decision. I have come across situations where the investor decided the next day to back out of the purchase, only to be told by their broker that it is too late and they now own the stock.

This is not true; investors have **Salutatory Rights.**

"These rights are for purchases on the primary market only, if the securities are issued in Canada under prospectus requirements:

- ***Right of Withdrawal** – within two business days after receipt of a prospectus, the purchaser can get out of the deal, no questions asked;*

- ***Right of Rescission** – must be brought within 180 days of the date of transaction and only if the prospectus contained a misrepresentation or material omission;*

- ***Right of Action for Damages** – if the investor is financially damaged because of a mis-representation or material omission, the investor may sue the issuer, the directors of the issuer, the investment advisor, the investment advisor's company, any expert* *(auditor, lawyer, geologist) whose mistake or misrepresentation damaged them financially;*[20]

"In every case, investors have burned themselves on IPOs, have stayed away for at least two years, but have always returned for another scalding. For as long as stock markets have existed, investors have gone through this manic-depressive cycle."[21]

- Benjamin Graham

Final Word

Here are some thoughts on **IPOs** from a few of the investing legends...

Warren Buffett is quoted making the following statements about **IPOs** at the following website:

https://www.safalniveshak.com/3-reasons-ipos-are-bad-investments/

[20] "Securities Act - *Bclaws.ca*." N.p., n.d. Web. 24 Aug. 2019 http://www.bclaws.ca/civix/document/id/complete/statreg/96418_01.
[21] The Intelligent Investor: https://www.amazon.in/gp/product/0062312685/ref=as_li_qf_sp_asin_il_tl?ie=UTF8&camp=3626&creative=24790&creativeASIN=0062312685&linkCode=as2&tag=safanive-21

In his 1993 letter, Buffett wrote…

> *"[An] intelligent investor in common stocks will do better in the secondary market than he will do buying new issues…[IPO] market is ruled by controlling stockholders and corporations, who can usually select the timing of offerings or, if the market looks unfavourable, can avoid an offering altogether. Understandably, these sellers are not going to offer any bargains, either by way of public offering or in a negotiated transaction."[22]*

When Buffett issued Class-B shares of Berkshire, he made sure that it wasn't a typical **IPO**. He wrote in his 1997 letter…

> *"Our issuance of the B shares not only arrested the sale of the trusts but provided a low-cost way for people to invest in Berkshire if they still wished to after hearing the warnings we issued.*
>
> *To blunt the enthusiasm that brokers normally have for pushing new issues—**because that's where the money is**—we arranged for our offering to carry a commission of only 1½%, the lowest payoff that we have ever seen in common stock underwriting.*

---

[22] "3 Reasons IPO's Are Almost Always Bad Investments | *Safal Niveshak*". N.p., n.d. Web. 23 Jul. 2019 https://www.safalniveshak.com/3-reasons-ipos-are-bad-investments/.

*Additionally, we made the amount of the offering open-ended, thereby repelling the typical **IPO** buyer who looks for a short-term price spurt arising from a combination of hype and scarcity."(ibid)*

The dot com crash of 2000 was preceded by hundreds of ***IPOs*** where the underlying business was literally nonexistent.

In his 2001 letter, Buffett wrote...

*"The fact is that a bubble market has allowed the creation of bubble companies, entities designed more with an eye to making money off investors rather than for them. Too often, an **IPO**, not profits, was the primary goal of a company's promoters.*

At bottom, the "business model" for these companies has been the old-fashioned chain letter, for which many fee-hungry investment bankers acted as eager postmen."(ibid)

Benjamin Graham wrote in Chapter 6 of ***The Intelligent Investor...***

*"Our one recommendation is that all investors should be wary of new issues—which means, simply, that these should be subjected to careful examination and unusually severe tests before they are purchased. There are two reasons for this double caveat. The first is that new issues[**IPO**]*

have special salesmanship behind them, which calls therefore for a special degree of sales resistance. The second is that most new issues are sold under "favorable market conditions"—which means favorable for the seller and consequently less favorable for the buyer." (ibid)

Charlie Munger said this in Berkshire's 2004 meeting…

*"It is entirely possible that you could use our mental models to find good **IPO**s to buy. There are countless **IPO**s every year, and I'm sure that there are a few cinches that you could jump on. But the average person is going to get creamed. So, if you're talented, good luck."* (ibid)

To which Buffett added…

*"An **IPO** is like a negotiated transaction – the seller chooses when to come public – and it's unlikely to be a time that's favorable to you. So, by scanning 100 **IPO**s, you're way less likely to find anything interesting than scanning an average group of 100 stocks."* (ibid)

Buffett also said…

"It's almost a mathematical impossibility to imagine that, out of the thousands of things for sale on a given day, the most attractively priced is the one being sold by a knowledgeable seller

(company insiders) to a less-knowledgeable buyer (investors)." (ibid)

The late Mr. Parag Parikh wrote in his book, ***Value Investing and Behaviour Finance...***

> *"It's safe to conclude that **IPO**s, which seem like a good investment vehicle are, in reality, not so. In fact, an **IPO** is a product which is against investor interest, as it is mostly offered to investors when they are willing to pay a higher and outrageous valuation in boom times." (ibid)*

Prof. Sanjay Bakshi wrote this in a 2000 article ...

> *"Any kind of rational comparison of long-term returns in the **IPO** market and the secondary market would show that investors do far better in the latter than in the former...**IPO**'s are one of the surest ways of losing money in the long run."*

> *Four characteristics of the **IPO** market makes it a market where it is far more profitable to be a seller than to be a buyer.*

> ***First,** in the **IPO** market, there are many buyers and only a handful of sellers.*

> ***Second**, the sellers, being insiders, always know more about the company whose shares are to be sold, than the buyers.*

Third, *the sellers hold an extremely valuable option of deciding the timing of the sale. Naturally, they would choose to sell only when they get high prices for the shares.*

Finally, the quantity of shares being offered is flexible and can be "managed" by the merchant bankers to attain the optimum price from the sellers' viewpoint. But what is "optimum" from the sellers' viewpoint is not the "optimum" from the buyers' viewpoint. This is an important point to note: Companies want to raise capital at the lowest possible cost, which from their viewpoint means issuance of shares at high prices. That is why bull markets are always accompanied by a surge in the issuance of shares." (ibid)

Trading as Agent

"An agency transaction is the other popular method for executing a client's orders. More complicated than regular principal transactions, these deals involve the search for and transfer of securities between clients of different brokerages. The increasing number of participants in the securities market and the need for extremely accurate bookkeeping, clearing, settlement, and reconciliation make ensuring the smooth flow of the securities markets quite a task."[23]

[23] "Principal Trading and Agency Trading - *Yahoo Finance*." N.p., n.d. Web. 23 Jul. 2019 https://finance.yahoo.com/news/principal-trading-agency-trading-170000752.html.

"An agency broker is a broker that acts as a middleman to the stock exchange, and places trades on behalf of clients. This is in direct contrast to broker-dealers, who purchase orders from clients and then sell these blocks into the market. Unlike the broker-dealer, **the agency broker must put its client interests first and work to achieve the best execution for the trade**. Special care must be taken when using any broker, as there may be hidden fees associated with placing trades. When interacting with a broker, it is always a good idea to ask the capacity in which they are functioning — as your agent or simply as a broker-dealer. This will tell you about where their focus and obligation lies when working your trades."[24]

2. Mutual Funds

To make their own lives easier and to attempt to treat their clients equally, financial advisors often suggest mutual funds rather than individual stocks and bonds.

---

[24] Kenton, Will. "Agency Broker." *Investopedia*, Investopedia, 12 Mar. 2019, https://www.investopedia.com/terms/a/agencybroker.asp.

This selection allows them to access the expertise and services of the mutual funds' professional investment management team.

This selection also reduces the advisors' workload in terms of research and client management. They can then provide you (their client) with the information and research data supplied **by the mutual fund companies (Sometimes this is self-serving data)**.

This selection is a somewhat better solution, as the responsibility for investment selection is now passed onto the mutual fund investment management team and doesn't rest on the individual stock picking ability of the advisor.

While this may be an improvement, some problems still exist.

Why? Your advisor must now research the thousands of mutual funds available for sale in Canada and suggest several for your consideration. This process is labour-intensive and can be a daunting task for the advisor as there are more mutual funds for sale than stocks listed on the Canadian Stock Exchanges.

Alternatively, the advisor may rely on their in-house research teams to recommend a mutual fund.

And advisors (stockbrokers) still must manage each client portfolio individually, just like a stock portfolio. Instead of recommending individual stocks and bonds, they are recommending individual mutual funds.

3. Private Money Management

The **third choice** and the one that I recommend is **Private Money Management**.

Private Money Management involves using professional *Portfolio Managers* to make the individual stock and bond decisions on your behalf.

This approach is more customized than simply buying mutual funds. This is the way many high net worth individuals and families have their money managed.

Portfolio Managers are individuals or firms that manage customized investment portfolios on behalf of foundations, pensions funds, endowments, financial institutions, and private clients.

Portfolio Managers differ from mutual fund advisors and stockbrokers because they are fiduciaries and generally have a higher level of education and qualification.

Portfolio Managers manage larger portfolios for fewer clients. They provide much more personalized management of investment portfolios that is not available with mutual fund advisors and stockbrokers. Since *Portfolio Managers* manage fewer and much larger portfolios, they often charge their clients lower management fees.

With *Portfolio Managers*, you get a dedicated investment management team. Their responsibility is to create *Optimized Portfolios* that maximize the expected return at a given level of risk.

They accomplish this by developing a written agreement known as an *Investment Policy Statement* or *(IPS)* that considers your specific investment needs and goals.

Your *IPS* forms the basis upon which your *Portfolio Managers* select an appropriate mix of investments and makes discretionary adjustments to your portfolio to optimize the asset mix and minimize the overall investment risk.

They employ strategies to make the necessary investment changes to all client portfolios at the same time, so clients large or small get exactly the same treatment at the same instant in time.

So unlike a stock broker, mutual fund advisor, or any other advisor that falls under the umbrella of a financial advisor, the investment management team can spend 100% of their time designing, building custom portfolios, and hiring the right managers to manage their client's money.

CHAPTER 7

QUESTION 6
FOR YOUR FINANCIAL ADVISOR

Do you have a process in place to automatically rebalance your clients' portfolios?

Rebalancing is an important aspect of your long-term investment strategy. It maintains your optimum asset mix, keeps your risk level in check, and ensures your portfolio stays on track.

Your portfolio should reflect your investment objectives, personal financial goals, and use the Investment Policy Statement to help you achieve your goals.

Over time, as different *Asset Classes* perform at different rates; your portfolio may deviate from your original asset allocation.

This means that your portfolio may no longer be performing

according to your Investment Plan, and you may be exposed to a greater level of risk than you are comfortable with.

Rebalancing is the process of buying and selling portions of your portfolio in order to reset the *Asset Classes* back to their original state. It serves to reduce risk, lock in gains, and impose discipline on the investment process.

Optimum Asset Mix

Off Strategy

Back on Strategy

Your *Family Wealth Advisor* and their investment management team should have a process in place that continuously monitors your portfolio to ensure that your asset allocation remains appropriate.

If any part of your portfolio deviates from its target allocation by more than a certain percentage, for example 10%, they should take appropriate steps to bring it back in line with its target weight. Breaking these thresholds could signal unnecessary portfolio risk or a lost investment opportunity.

The following chart illustrates how various *Asset Classes* performed differently each year, creating opportunities to rebalance your portfolio to optimize your portfolio returns.

The assets at the top of the chart are the best performing assets for that year, while the assets at the bottom of the chart are the worst-performing asset for that year. As you can see, they change positions every year.

This presents ***Portfolio Managers*** the opportunity to rebalance your portfolio as they sell portions of the out-performing assets and invest them into the underperforming assets to bring your portfolio back to its original target asset mix as dictated by your ***Investment Policy Statement***.

Annual Returns for 20 Major Asset Classes

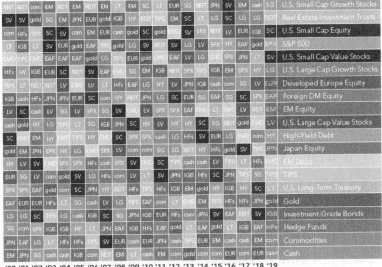

'00 '01 '02 '03 '04 '05 '06 '07 '08 '09 '10 '11 '12 '13 '14 '15 '16 '17 '18 '19
Source: Fidelity[25]

Regular rebalancing may help you to achieve better risk-adjusted long-term returns because it automatically leverages the discipline of "buying low and selling high" by realigning your assets from those that have performed exceptionally well to other areas of your portfolio that have lagged.

[25] "Kiss — *Greater Fool – Authored by Garth Turner – The Troubled Future of Real Estate*" N.p., n.d. Web. 26 Jul. 2019 https://www.greaterfool.ca/2019/05/25/kiss-2/

While it is impossible to predict which *Asset Classe* will outperform at any given time, rebalancing ensures that your portfolio is always poised to take advantage of the next market cycle.

Automatic rebalancing takes the emotion out of buy and sell decisions, which can be affected by short-term market events and keeps you focused on your long-term investment strategy.

Rebalancing helps to ensure that your investments always reflect your personal goals and investment profile, so you are not subject to the whims of random investment decisions or rumours.

Without a plan, you may be influenced into buying a security or stock because someone you trust tells you to buy it because they tell you it's a good investment or to sell it because they told you to sell. There may be little or no research behind your decision to purchase or sell the security - just someone's opinion or a rumour.

When you have an investment plan in place and your portfolio is rebalanced regularly to maintain your portfolio's targeted asset mix based on your risk profile, you are less likely to be influenced by rumours and make random investment decisions.

CHAPTER 8

QUESTION 7
FOR YOUR FINANCIAL ADVISOR

Do you offer Asset Class portfolio diversification?

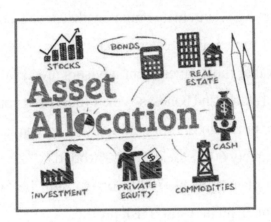

It's important to have a widely diversified portfolio to maximize investment returns while reducing overall market and stock risk.

No single investment is right for every point in time.

A properly constructed portfolio is needed to help smooth out the market's ups and downs.

The key is diversification. By combining different styles of investments, different *Asset Classes*, and exposure to various geographic regions, your portfolio would be positioned to grow to its full potential.

Diversification provides more consistent and predictable returns by lessening the effects of any one single investment on overall portfolio performance.

Stocks and Bonds

I believe it is extremely important that people understand how their money is invested on an ongoing basis. One of the keys that most investment advisors always discuss is the mix of stocks and bonds, so when you look at your typical Canadian portfolio or mutual fund, you will have a mix of approximately 60% stocks and 40% bonds.

This mix might be 70/30, or it might be 50/50; all dependent on an investor's risk profile.

However, there is a major problem with this model.

I believe that this portfolio model is broken.

TYPICAL PORTFOLIO

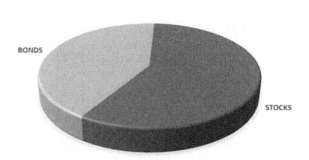

The main draw to this strategy is in its simplicity. Most advisors believe that diversification of stocks and bonds is key to reducing portfolio risk and volatility. This view of diversification has seen some changes. The investing environment now has low yielding bonds offering a negative real rate of return after adjusting for inflation. Bonds are at risk of dropping in value as interest rates rise. In addition, we are at all-time stock market highs globally with a high probability of a market correction in the near term. This historical combination of stocks and bonds offered protection in the past because bonds values went up as stocks went down and protected a portfolio in a stock market downturn.

Source: FactSet. Data as of 12/31/17[26]

[26] "New Client Assets in Today's Market: A Blessing or a Curse?" *Paritas Capital Management*, 6 Apr. 2018, https://www.paritascapital.com/blog/new-client-assets-in-todays-market-a-blessing-or-a-curse/.

Bonds offered this protection since the peak of the interest rate cycle in 1980.

There was very little risk of bonds losing money since bond values increased as interest rates dropped. The reverse will now happen as interest rates start to rise and bond values fall, making bonds riskier than stocks going forward.

As a result, bonds no longer offer the protection to offset stock losses they once did.

Warren Buffet said it best; fixed income long term is actually the riskiest *Asset Class* that you can own today because after inflation, currency and interest rate risk, you will guarantee yourself a loss long term. You need fixed income in your portfolio for income-generating needs, and especially for retirees you need it for protection against downside risk, and you also need it for when the stock market falls so that you can sell off those bonds to buy reasonably priced to lower than average priced equities that you want to own.

> *"It is a terrible mistake for investors with long-term horizons – among them, pension funds, college endowments, and savings-minded individuals — to measure their investment 'risk' by their portfolio's ratio of bonds to stocks. Often, high-grade bonds in an investment portfolio increase its risk."[27]*
>
> *- Warren Buffett*

[27] Buffett: 'I Would Choose Equities In A Minute' Over Bonds." *CNBC.com* N.p., n.d. Web. 02 Aug. 2019 https://www.cnbc.com/2018/02/26/buffett-when-choosing-between-stocks-and-bonds-i-would-choose-equities-in-a-minute.html
.

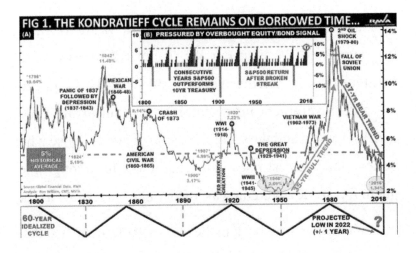

Source: William, Ron. "Goldilocks & The Big Bond Bear: Deflationary Spike Risk Into 4%." *LinkedIn*[28]

The above chart shows historical interest rates back to 1800. The chart clearly shows that interest rates move in approximately 60-year cycles. 30 years up and 30 years down with a long-term average of 5%. So, given this historical information and the fact we are now at historically low rates, you can fairly safely deduct that interest rates are on the verge of starting the next 30 year upcycle. This is bad news for bonds as bond values drop when interest rates rise. This is also bad news for stocks as stocks underperform during periods of rising interest rates.

[28] William, Ron. "GOLDILOCKS & THE BIG BOND BEAR: DEFLATIONARY SPIKE RISK INTO 4%."*LinkedIn* , https://www.linkedin.com/pulse/goldilocks-big-bond-bear-deflationary-spike-risk-4-ron/

As you can see from the previous chart, we are living on borrowed time. We are in our 38th year of a downward trend in interest rates when the average is 30 years. This is due to massive government intervention as a result of the 2000 tech meltdown and the great recession of 2007. Those who believe that interest rates will remain low for a long time are in for a rude awakening as history always repeats itself.

Yale University, back in the early 1980s, identified that a pure stock and bond model does not offer enough downside protection, and a better model was needed. They and many other *Portfolio Managers* have talked about this. They believed the key to investing is not necessarily diversification in the traditional sense of a portfolio of hundreds of stocks and bonds. You need diversification of multiple non-correlating *Asset Classes* , meaning, for example, in addition to stocks and bonds, you need to add *Alternate Asset Classes.*

In a recent article in Advisoranalyst.com, Guy Haselmann, Macro Strategist, talks about *"The Death of the 60/40 Portfolio."*

> *"After almost 70 years of success, the 60/40 portfolio investment approach has become too risky and structurally **incapable** of meeting its intended objectives. It needs revisiting...*

*Foundations of the 60/40 portfolio emerged from Harry Markowitz's Modern Portfolio Theory (MPT) work in the 1950s, which won him the Nobel Prize. It is also the **basis** on which today's Robo-advising algorithms are written. Yet, MPT never envisioned a world where someone has to pay to lend money."*

Haselmann continues:

*"For over a half-century, the two-asset 60/40 stock and bond portfolio **did** an excellent job providing the four main goals of a sound portfolio: 1. growth, 2. inflation-protection, 3. income and 4. down-side protection.*

Stocks would typically benefit over time from the first two objectives and bonds from the latter two.

*There is no doubt that realized returns from 60/40-type portfolios have **been** extraordinary; and, even more so in recent years, due to the "**Everything Bubble**"- which is the result of excessive accommodation from global central banks.*

The strategy has provided a wonderful, convenient, and easy way to structure a simple portfolio and still achieve the intended objectives of the portfolio. However, bonds have been in a bull market since 1982 and may have reached their **practical** *limits and US stock market capitalization has risen to an astounding 164% of GDP...*

The 60/40 strategy is now looking ineffectual and too risky. *Stated differently, a diversified, but long-only, mix of stocks and bonds, is no longer a safe, balanced, or prudent portfolio structure."*

He warns:

"After 11 years of financial repression and wild market speculation, the setting is **ripe** *for a "Minsky Moment" whereby stocks and bonds snap violently lower without central banks having the power to stop or prevent the crash..."*

His conclusion:

*"**All** bubbles eventually pop. Fear of missing the upside of a bigger stock and bond bubble fueled by central bank actions is a poor strategy, as well as being reckless and unwise.*

When building or adjusting a portfolio, the question an investor should be asking is: "How can I achieve my life's goals and my portfolio objectives with some degree of certainty?" Stocks and bonds represent only a small **sliver** *of the investable landscape.*

*There are hundreds of **alternative** investment exposures that investors can choose from today, many of which were not available in the past. Some examples include long/short strategies, peer-to-peer lending, TIPS, royalties, venture capital, or real investment strategies, to name a few.*

*In short, investors should seek a diversified portfolio whose components and exposures are non- or less-correlated and more **idiosyncratic**."[29]*

The 60/40 Portfolio Is Riskier Than Ever

It seems that every analyst and investment firm spends many hours staring into their respective crystal balls and chicken entrails to divine the future of the markets. They make assumptions and prognostications to guide their decisions.

---

[29]"The Death Of The 60/40 Portfolio – *Advisor Analysist.com*" N.p., n.d. Web. 24 Aug. 2019 https://advisoranalyst.com/2019/08/19/guy-haselmann-the-death-of-the-60-40-portfolio.html/

What does the future hold?

"Danger, Will Robinson!"

*(from the 1960's TV series **Lost in Space**)*

John Mauldin of RealInvestmentadvice.com agrees with Haselmann and writes as follows:

> *"As investors, we have to make assumptions about the future. We know they will likely prove wrong, but something has to guide our asset allocation decisions.*
>
> *Many long-term investors assume stocks will give them 6–8% real annual returns if they simply buy and hold long enough.*
>
> *Those reassurances are increasingly hollow, thanks to both low rates and inflated stock valuations, yet people running massive piles of money behave as if they are unquestionably correct.*
>
> *The point is that returns in the next 7 or 10 years will not look anything like the past."* [30]

---

[30] "Mauldin: The 60/40 Portfolio Is Riskier Than Ever." *Zero Hedge*, https://www.zerohedge.com/markets/mauldin-6040-portfolio-riskier-ever.

The GMO Asset Allocation team agrees and produced a 7-year *Asset Class Forecast* that is somewhat less than optimistic.

They see this longest bull market ever, (two decades) coming to a close. Whether a slowdown or a crash, they see growth slowing and even reversing.

US stocks and bonds are projected to be in negative territory.

7-YEAR ASSET CLASS REAL RETURN FORECASTS*

As of August 31, 2019

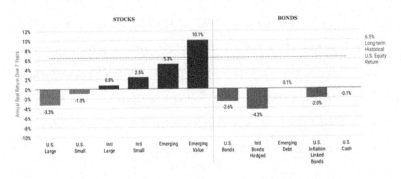

Source: GMO, Mauldin: The 60/40 Portfolio Is Riskier Than Ever[31]

[31]"GMO 7-Year Asset Class Forecast: August 2019."*Home,* https://www.gmo.com/americas/research-library/gmo-7-year-asset-class-forecast-august-2019/

The 60/40 Fallacy

Mauldin continues:

> *"Many financial advisors, apparently unaware the event horizon is near, continue to recommend old solutions like the "60/40" portfolio.*
>
> *That strategy does have a compelling history. Those who adopted and actually stuck with it (which is very hard)* **had several good decades**. *That doesn't guarantee them several more, though. I believe times have changed.*
>
> *When (not if) we have a recession and the stock market drops 40% or more, index investors will have spent 20 years with a less than* **1% compound annual return**. *A 50% drop, which could certainly happen in a recession, would wipe out all their gains, even without inflation.*
>
> *The "logic" of 60/40 is that it gives you diversification. The bonds should perform well when the stocks run into difficulty, and vice versa. You might even get lucky and have both components rise together. But you can also be unlucky and see them both fall, an outcome I think increasingly likely.*

*So, 60/40 could keep firing on all cylinders for a while. But it won't do so forever, and the **ending will probably be sudden and spectacular**.* " [ibid]

Mauldin asserts:

*"The primary investment goal as we approach the recession should be **"Hold on to what you have."** Or, in other words, capital preservation."* [ibid]

As we look at potential losses in the future, here are some numbers that very few people (including *Wealth Advisors* and *Portfolio Managers* emphasize or even discuss.

If your portfolio drops by 20%, you will need future gains of **25% ... just to break even!**

A portfolio drop of 30% requires a future gain of **43% just to break even!**

A portfolio drop of 40% requires a future gain of **67% just to break even!**

A portfolio drop of 50% means your portfolio must earn 100% **just to break even!**

Let's run some numbers!

If your portfolio drops **30%** in the next downturn, you will need to earn **6%** per year for the next **7** $^{1/2}$ **(SEVEN-AND-A-HALF)** years just to bring your portfolio up to where it was before the downturn! Will we see those 6-8% annual returns going forward?

Montecito Capital Management writes on their website:

*"Most investment advisors are not **Portfolio Managers**. For all intents and purposes, a large body of financial advisors profess the success of a buy-and-hold investment strategy and do not actively manage your assets. However, if you are retired or are near retirement, a well thought out portfolio adjustment plan and sell discipline becomes all the more important. Your nest egg is likely a great source of your retirement livelihood, and your financial advisor has based "average annual" returns on much longer time-horizons that are positive for the rest of your retirement - **this is complacency management (not active) and is pure speculation**. Upon retirement, you will likely begin taking income from your retirement portfolio based on your needs and what your adviser believes to be prudent.*

WHO'S INVESTING YOUR MONEY?

This "reverse dollar-cost averaging" often occurs when you no longer have the luxury of a long-term investment horizon. The most important risk in your portfolio is time, particularly the decay of opportunities for a greater total return, or more time to recover from a potential market loss as you hit your golden years. [32]

To offset the inherent risk of a simple 60/40, buy and hold portfolio strategy, you will need a different strategy to preserve your portfolio in a market downturn.

In addition to **Stocks** and **Bonds**, you need to add **Alternative Asset Classes** that act opposite to **Stocks** and **Bonds** in your portfolio.

I will discuss this in more detail later in this chapter.

---

[32] "Portfolio Asset Allocation Investing Strategies Santa Barbara & Los Angeles Asset Manager I How to Invest, How to Protect Your Portfolio from Loss Risks & Free Investing Advice Stocks, Bonds, Alternative Assets." *Montecito Capital Management I Building Brighter Futures*, https://www.mcapitalmgt.com/portfolio.html.

Before we go there, I need to address the misconception about stock diversification.

Public Stocks

When most advisors talk about diversification, they talk about the diversification of stocks. Academic researchers suggest that when you have 20 - 30 different equities (or stock positions) in your portfolio, you have decreased specific stock risk to near zero. By continually adding more stocks (or equities) above 30 to your portfolio, you do not reduce the risk of the portfolio in any significant manner.[33]

*"In his influential 1949 book, **The Intelligent Investor**, Benjamin Graham argued that a portfolio of 10 to 30 stocks provides adequate diversification. Mr. Graham didn't pick stocks at random, of course. He subjected them to careful scrutiny and insisted on buying them at a price that provided a "margin of safety," thus complementing the benefits of diversification.*

---

[33] "Staff, Investopedia. "What is the Ideal Number of Stocks to Have in a Portfolio?"*Investopedia*, 11 July 2019, www.investopedia.com/ask/answers/05/optimalportfoliosize.asp

The academics disagree over how many separate stocks are required to secure the benefits of diversification, but most professionally managed equity portfolios have at least 30 or so individual securities in them," U.S. fund manager Daniel Peris wrote in his 2011 book, **The Strategic Dividend Investor.** *"*[34]

"As legendary investor Peter Lynch pointed out, "investors should be aware of negative consequences when their portfolios consist of too many stocks. After all, there is no point in constructing a portfolio with large quantities of holdings as one can simply buy an ETF that closely mimics the selected strategy benchmark."[35]

What happens with the typical mutual fund portfolio is they hold on average between 90 – 120 different stock positions. What they have essentially created is a certain market index, whether it be the Dow Jones, the NASDAQ or S&P 500 or the TSX.

---

[34] "How Many Stocks Do I Need for a Diversified Portfolio?" *The Globe and Mail*, 12 May 2018, www.theglobeandmail.com/globe-investor/investor-education/how-many-stocks-do-i-need-for-a-diversified-portfolio/article19165150/.
[35] Krejca, David. "How Many Stocks Make Up A Well-Diversified Portfolio?" *Seeking Alpha*, 16 Sept. 2016, https://seekingalpha.com/article/4006697-many-stocks-make-well-diversified-portfolio.

So, why would an investor pay a management fee of 2% to 2.75% to their investment advisor when they can get the same investment by buying a Vanguard S&P 500 Exchange Traded Fund (ETF) for about 30 basis points (.3%). Essentially, they will get the same investment return without paying significant management fees.

This ongoing management fee was one of the major downsides identified with owning a portfolio of mutual funds.

What About Mutual Funds?

Many investors are novices at picking individual stocks, and over the years, many have lost their shirt – remember Bre-X in 1997, Enron in 2001, Worldcom in 2002, Bear Stearns and Lehman Brothers in 2008, Nortel in 2009 and Theranos in 2016?

These are just a few of the largest stock market failures that bankrupted large and small investors over the years.

"In 1932, the first Canadian mutual fund was established and by 1951 had assets of $51 million.

The growth of mutual funds and their impact on investing, in general, was nothing short of revolutionary.

*For the first time, **ordinary investors with minimal capital** could pool their resources in a professionally managed, diversified basket of investments, rather than going the more expensive route of buying individual stocks of varying risks. This was considered a giant step in the democratization of investments for the average person.*"[36]

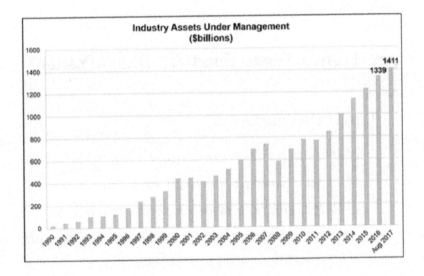

Source: The History of Mutual Funds | Ific.ca." *Investment Funds Institute of Canada*[37]

36, 37 "The History Of Mutual Funds | Ific.ca." *Investment Funds Institute of Canada.* N.p., n.d. Web. 01 Aug. 2019 https://www.ific.ca/en/articles/who-we-are-history-of-mutual-funds/.

The investors didn't have to be sophisticated, and they could buy shares in the mutual fund on a monthly basis. In the 1980s and 1990s, many funds saw incredible returns, and investment in these funds hit a record high.

The bursting of the Tech Bubble in 2000 and the Great Recession of 2007 scared people away from mutual funds and into real estate. They are once again growing with tens of thousands of funds holding trillions of dollars in assets under management.

Are Mutual Funds Good for Diversification?

David LeNeveu writes:

> *"If you are like the majority of investors in Canada, your portfolio of investments in your RRSPs, TFSAs, and other accounts likely hold a number of mutual funds as picked by yourself, suggested by a friend, or recommended to you by an advisor.*
>
> *Likely, you have been told that by having different mutual funds, you are well diversified and have not given it another thought (other than to make sure they are performing).*

While it is true that as an investor, you need to hold a number of different stocks (equities) to be properly diversified, the question very few think to ask is, 'Can I be over-diversified?'

The quick answer, YES! To begin, we need to remember that the idea behind diversification, simply put, is to reduce risk while maximizing return. At its core, this is a very simple concept. Academically speaking, a portfolio of just 32 stocks will reduce the overall specific risk (non-systematic) of a portfolio by 95%. By adding another stock, you are no longer achieving any more significant reduction in risk. [38]

You may actually now be suffering from "diworsification."

This term was coined by Peter Lynch, a legendary fund manager who published the book, One Up on Wall Street. He wrote that "a business (or portfolio) that diversifies too widely risks destroying itself because management time, energy, and resources are diverted from the original investment. [39]

[38] How Many Stocks Do I Need for a Diversified Portfolio?" *The Globe and Mail*, 12 May 2018, www.theglobeandmail.com/globe-investor/investor-education/how-many-stocks-do-i-need-for-a-diversified-portfolio/article19165150/.

[39] Krejca, David. "How Many Stocks Make Up A Well-Diversified Portfolio?" *Seeking Alpha*, 16 Sept. 2016, https://seekingalpha.com/article/4006697-many-stocks-make-well-diversified-portfolio.

So why then, would your typical mutual fund hold well over 32 stocks? Unfortunately, it may be because mutual fund managers are looking out for their own best interest, instead of yours. Mutual fund managers' jobs and paycheques depend on their performance as compared to a benchmark, index and/ or to each other. If a mutual fund manager can achieve a return that is close to the benchmark, they can reasonably feel secure and justify their job and paycheque. This structure encourages and enables mutual fund managers to simply pick enough equities to closely mirror the benchmark they are being compared to (a term called **closet indexing**.[40]

This brings us back to our typical Canadian investor. If a typical mutual fund holds an average portfolio of 90 stocks and you hold even just 3 or 4 mutual funds, you likely have a portfolio that holds well over 200 different stocks.

You have now just fundamentally bought a benchmark or index fund. After fees and taxes that are passed from the fund to the investor, our outcome is, inevitably, **underperformance**.

---

[40] Chen, James. "Closet Indexing." *Investopedia*, Investopedia, 21 July 2019, www.investopedia.com/terms/c/closetindexing.asp

This is further compounded when our investor finally does decide to move between advisors (independent or the bank) because of poor performance, relationship, trust, fees, etc. The new advisor will now usually suggest three, four, or more different mutual funds.

Unfortunately, this essentially gives the investor an almost identical overall underlying investment. The investor feels positive about making a change, but very little change has actually occurred.

Ultimately, there is no point in paying the cost of a mutual fund manager and all of the embedded fees when you can simply and cheaply buy essentially the same thing with a passively held index or benchmark ETF (Exchange Traded Fund).

Don't get me wrong; I am not saying that you should just go buy a passively invested index ETF (though in some cases it is the right answer). I am a believer, proponent, and investor of a fully discretionary, actively managed, properly designed portfolio. I encourage all investors to carefully review their portfolio, its investments and how it is being managed. "[41]

[41] "The Problem with Mutual Funds | *Rockmoor Wealth Management*." N.p., n.d. Web. 16 Jul. 2019 https://rockmoorwealth.com/the-problem-with-mutual-funds/

Are ETF's a better investment alternative to Mutual Funds?

"In 2003, Warren Buffett called derivatives weapons of mass destruction. Borrowing Buffett's terminology, Arik Ahitov and Dennis Bryan, FPA Capital fund managers, call ETFs "weapons of mass destruction" that have distorted stock prices and created the potential for a market selloff.

According to JPM's Nikolaos Panigirtzoglou, the takeover by ETFs really means that:

- ***Markets become riskier:*** *"The shift towards passive funds has the potential to concentrate investments to a few large products. This concentration potentially increases systemic risk making markets more susceptible to the flows of a few large passive products."*

- ***Passive or index investing favours large-caps as most equity indices are market cap-weighted:*** *"This could exacerbate the flow into large companies beyond to what is justified by fundamentals, creating a potential misallocation of capital away from smaller companies. To the extent that these* *passive funds become even more dominant in the future, the risk of bubbles being formed in large companies, at the same time crowding out investments from smaller firms, would significantly increase."*

- **Crashes, when they happen, will be bigger and worse:** *"The shift towards passive funds tends to intensify following periods of strong market performance as active managers underperform in such periods of strong market performance. In turn, this shift exacerbates the market uptrend creating more protracted periods of low volatility and momentum. When markets eventually reverse, the correction becomes deeper, and volatility rises."*

- **Markets become less efficient:** *"If passive investing becomes too big, potentially crowding out skilled, active managers also, market efficiency would start declining. In turn, this would present opportunities for active managers."*[42]

---

[42] The Belgian Dentist Portfolio. "What To Do When ETFs Become Weapons Of Mass Destruction?" *Seeking Alpha,* 10 June 2018, https://seekingalpha.com/article/4180604-etfs-become-weapons-mass-destruction

Why is diversification important?

Diversification, also known as spreading the risk; **PROTECTS** your investment.

You are not putting all your eggs into one basket. Kicking over the basket jeopardizes all the eggs.

In the same way, having all your money tied up in one stock or mutual fund or one country could be disastrous to your financial health.

For example, many Canadians have not saved for retirement and have all their money tied up in their homes. They are hoping that at some point in time, they will be able to cash out and use the money for their retirement.

Chapter 9 details why this One Asset Strategy may be a bad idea.

Typically, Canadian advisors tend to create portfolios concentrated heavily in Canadian stocks and bonds with only some diversification into US and international stocks and with **NO** diversification into *Alternate Asset Classes*. This asset mix may increase the risk to the portfolio significantly.

Why? Because a large percentage of the Canadian Index is resource-based (oil, gas, and mining stocks). If these sectors and companies take a beating because of the drop in international oil and commodity prices, your portfolio will take a severe beating.

With Canada representing less than 2% of the global economic opportunities, being heavily invested in Canadian securities means you are missing out on global opportunities and maybe taking on **WAY TOO MUCH** risk.

What might a diversified portfolio look like?

A typical portfolio might be diversified by:

Security type - stocks, bonds, and income trusts;

Geographic region - Canada, the U.S. and the rest of the world;

Company size - large and small market capitalization;

Investment style - value and growth.

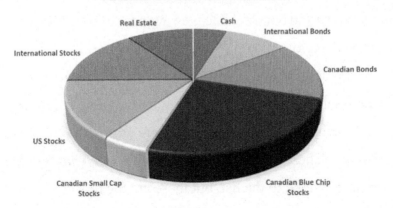

POSSIBLE DIVERSIFIED PORTFOLIO

While the previous image portfolio may look like a well-diversified portfolio, each of the assets depicted in the portfolio above can be broadly classified into two general *Asset Classes,* public *Stocks* and *Bonds*.

While Canadian, US, and International Stocks have a low correlation to each other, they are similar in nature and can, therefore, be classified as one *Asset Class "Stocks"* or *"Public Equity*." In a major market correction, they all tend to be affected somewhat similarly to the downside, offering minimal downside protection.

The same holds true for Canadian, US, and International Bonds; they are also similar in nature and can be classified as one *Asset Class "Bonds*." Since bonds offer historically low returns, they are at risk of declining in value as interest rates eventually rise, offering little portfolio protection in an inflationary environment.

If you look back at the GMO Chart on page 87, holding just stocks and bonds will leave your portfolio trending into negative regions.

This is where you will need to add *Alternative Asset Classes* that are distinctly different from *Stocks* and *Bonds*. Two such *Asset Classes* are *"Private Equity"* and *"Real Estate*." There are other *Alternative Asset Classes* that could be added to the list, but these are the most common.

These additional *Alternative Asset Classes* help smooth out portfolio volatility without sacrificing portfolio returns as as they usually move in different directions to *Public Stocks* and *Bonds.*

Portfolios that do not include *Alternative Asset Classes* do not offer true portfolio diversification in today's investment environment.

Having multiple assets of Canadian, US, and International stocks and Canadian, US, and International Bonds means that the investor is staying in two *Asset Classes*: *Stocks* and *Bonds.* That cannot be classified as diversification.

In a Globe and Mail Article titled "*Market timing and your retirement: Understanding the impact,*" Paul De Sousa had this to say:

> "*Over the last few decades, correlations between equities and fixed income are rising, negating the diversification benefits that these Asset Classes previously offered. A 60% equity, 40% fixed income portfolio does not offer meaningful diversification as it is an outdated simplified estimate of a balanced portfolio. Further diversification is available by style, sector, geography, capitalization, maturity, rating, and class. Despite this, the Asset Classes have not changed as equities and fixed income remain.*

*What is required to fully diversify portfolios is the use of **Alternative Asset Classes** such as **Private Equity**, private debt, **Real Estate**, natural resources, precious metals, hedge funds, and infrastructure. Allocating to this complete range of **Asset Classes** is referred to as the Endowment Model. Institutional and high net worth investors have adopted this model because the managers of these **Asset Classes** are less constrained, and the markets are more efficient. They also provide adequate returns during periods of low and negative real interest rates, while offering a low correlation to public markets. As a result, volatility can be smoothed, resulting in less intense losses.* "[43]

What Is an Alternative Investment?

"An alternative investment is a financial asset that does not fall into one of the conventional investment categories. Conventional categories include stocks, bonds, and cash. Most alternative investment assets are held by institutional investors or accredited, high-net-worth individuals because of their complex nature." [44]

[43]"Market Timing and Your Retirement: Understanding the Impact." *The Globe and Mail*, 5 Sept. 2019, https://www.theglobeandmail.com/investing/personal-finance/retirement/article-how-to-mitigate-the-risks-of-a-market-plunge-in-early-retirement/

[44] Alternative Investment Definition - *Investopedia*." N.p., n.d. Web. 17 Jul. 2019 https://www.investopedia.com/terms/a/alternative_investment.asp.

NON TRADITIONAL ASSET CLASS PORTFOLIO

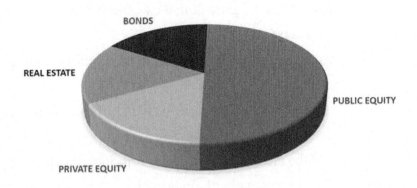

Why Alternative Assets?

> *"Alternative investments include **Private Equity** or **Venture Capital, Hedge Funds, Managed Futures, Art and Antiques, Commodities,** and **Derivatives Contracts.***
>
> ***Real Estate, in various forms,** is also often classified as an alternative investment."* (ibid)

PriceWaterhouseCoopers (PwC) writing in its report ***Alternative Asset Management 2020 - Fast forward to centre stage*** makes a credible case for increased and sustainable long-term investment returns using *Alternative Asset Classes*.

They note that asset managers are moving their assets to these alternative classes to improve their long-term returns that aren't tied to traditional **Stock** and **Bond** portfolios.

This report details the strategies these firms are using and what is behind the growth in these *Asset Classes*.

PwC asserts:

"Growth in assets will be driven principally by three key trends:

1. a government-incentivised shift to individual retirement plans;
2. the increase of high-net-worth-individuals from emerging populations; and
3. the growth of sovereign investors.

This creates the need for more tailored, outcome-based alternative products that provide capital preservation, but provide upside opportunities."[45]

In an op-ed article titled "*Why the democratization of alternative investments needs to accelerate,*" Barry McInerney, President, and CEO of Mackenzie Investments had this to say:

"*In fact, our largest Canadian public pension plans have led the way in investing in alternatives, such as* **Real Estate, Private Equity**, *infrastructure, commodities, and absolute return strategies, with typical allocations ranging from 30 % to 50 %.*

[45] "Moving Centre Stage: Alternative Asset Management In 2020." *The Alternative Investment Management Association (AIMA)*. N.p., n.d. Web. 24 Aug. 2019 https://www.aima.org/journal/aima-journal—q4-2015-edition/article/moving-centre-stage—alternative-asset-management-in-2020.html

Direct alternative investments have grown globally from US$2-trillion to US$15-trillion this century. This democratization needs to accelerate if Canadians are to maximize their retirement income. Further, access to these types of investments for retail investors will be even more crucial as we reach the later stages of a historic stock market bull run, possibly resulting in more modest returns from the public markets for equities - and perhaps even fixed income - over the next decade than the previous ten years.

Alternative Investments *– investments that either make use of sophisticated stock market strategies or invest in non-equity assets like **Real Estate** and infrastructure - can be very effective portfolio building blocks.*

They offer expanded investment return opportunities and lower correlations to traditional equity and fixed income markets and aim to achieve higher risk-adjusted returns over time.

*Canadian investors could benefit from gaining access to these types of **Asset Classes** to help ensure a smoother journey towards retirement and have more security after they retire too."*[46]

[46] McInerney, Barry. "Why the Democratization of Alternative Investments Needs to Accelerate." *The Globe and Mail*, The Globe and Mail, 4 Sept. 2019, https://www-theglobeandmail-com.cdn.ampproject.org/c/s/www.theglobeandmail.com/amp/investing/investment-ideas/article-why-the-democratization-of-alternative-investments-needs-to-accelerate/

The Modern Alternative Assets Landscape

*"A growing body of evidence suggests that greater exposure to **Alternative Assets** can boost portfolio returns and offer downside protection alongside a portfolio of traditional assets.*

*The general case for greater exposure to **Alternative Assets** is simple: due to their lower correlation with public markets, diversifying into alternatives can reduce a portfolio's overall exposure to risk."*[47]

Recall the ***Efficient Frontier*** chart in ***Chapter 4***, by adding ***Alternative Assets*** to a portfolio in the chart below; the ***Efficient Frontier*** is pushed upwards. The addition of ***Alternative Assets*** effectively restores the expected long-term returns a pure stock and bond portfolio once offered, without adding additional risk to the portfolio.

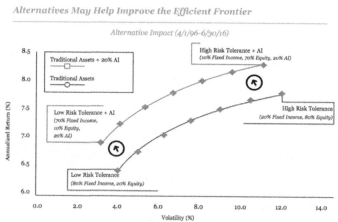

Alternatives May Help Improve the Efficient Frontier

Source: *EQUITYMULTIPLE*, "Alternative Assets in the Modern Portfolio." *(ibid)*
[47] "Alternative Assets in the Modern Portfolio." *EQUITYMULTIPLE*, 20 Aug. 2019, https://www.equitymultiple.com/blog/investing-strategy/alternative-assets

Let's now look at an outstanding investment model that has returned an unparalleled 13.0 percent compound annual return over the past 30 years as of June 30th, 2018.[48]

The Yale and Harvard Asset Allocation Model Explained

The Model was Developed by Yale and Harvard in the Mid-1980s

When Yale and Harvard started doing their investment studies in the 1980s, they understood that they managed millions of dollars in their endowment funds. They knew that long term the stock market has done great for everybody, but there is a lot of volatility in the market. Their whole management goal was not necessarily diversification, but it was trying to achieve what is called a *"risk-adjusted rate of return."* The question was, how were they going to achieve that return." They practiced diversification of *"Asset Classes."*

They moved beyond *Stocks* and *Bonds* and they went out into other *Alternative Asset Classes* such as *Private Equity* and *Real Estate*.

---

[48] "Home." *Yale Investments Office*, http://investments.yale.edu/home-1.

*"Yale's heavy allocation to non-traditional **Asset Classes** stems from their return potential and diversifying power. Today's actual and target portfolios have significantly higher expected returns and lower volatility. "**Alternative Assets**," by their very nature, tend to be less efficiently priced than traditional marketable securities, providing an opportunity to exploit market inefficiencies through active management."*[49]

"Yale's portfolio is structured using a combination of academic theory and informed market judgment. The theoretical framework relies on mean-variance analysis, an approach developed by Nobel laureates James Tobin and Harry Markowitz, both of whom conducted work on this important portfolio management tool at Yale's Cowles Foundation."[50]

[49] "Our Strategy — Yale Investments Office." N.p., n.d. Web. 12 Jul. 2019 http://investments.yale.edu/our-strategy-2/
[50] "Yale's Strategy — *Yale Investments Office.*" N.p., n.d. Web. 01 Aug. 2019 http://investments.yale.edu/about-the-yio/.

What are Public and Private Pension Funds Doing?

Public Pension Funds Turn to Alternative Asset Classes

> *"By 2020, there will be a fundamental shift towards alternatives by many sovereign and public pension funds. This is the continuation of a trend that first gained traction in the US and then globally. In April 2015, for instance, the world's largest pension fund, the $1.1tn Government Pension Investment Fund (GPIF) of Japan, announced a new strategic asset mix in a bid to achieve higher returns and address the needs of an aging population."[51]*

Why Does CPP Invest in Alternatives?

For years there was a concern that the Canada Pension Plan (CPP) would run out of money. This was before the CPP turned to "*Alternative Assets*." Today, Canada's biggest pension fund has embraced "*Alternative Assets*" and is no longer at risk of running out of money."

[51] "Alternative Asset Management 2020 - Fast Forward to Centre ..." PwC. N.p., n.d. Web. 17 Jul. 2019 https://www.pwc.com/jg/en/publications/alternative-asset-management-2020.pdf.

"There was a time when the Canada Pension Plan Investment Board didn't even make "alternative" investments. Now, Canada's biggest pension fund says it is sifting through "alternative" forms of data to try to improve its investment decisions."[52]

"Alternative Assets" generally have a low correlation to standard *Asset Classes* such as *Stocks* and *Bonds*. This means they often move counter to the *Stock* and *Bond* markets. This low correlation makes *"Alternative Assets"* suitable for maintaining a portfolio's long-term return while reducing portfolio risk.

This low correlation is just a fancy way of saying that the *Asset Classes* behave differently in the same market.

For example, if you could pick two investments that have relatively the same long-term return, but they peak and valley at different times, you can significantly reduce the day to day volatility of your portfolio.

The added diversification of unique and distinct *Asset Classes* again allows the long-term plan to meet its objectives through the interaction of the various *Asset Classes*.

---

[52] Zochodne, Geoff. "How CPPIB Is Tapping 'Alternative Data' to Refine Its Investment Processes." *Financial Post*, 18 Mar. 2019, https://business.financialpost.com/news/fp-street/how-cppib-is-tapping-alternative-data-to-refine-its-investment-processes.

When picking the right *Asset Classes*, you want to look for ones that are negatively correlated, meaning that they move in opposite directions to each other.

However, it is impossible to find investments that are perfectly opposite, but you want to find ones that are close.

The following chart illustrates two different *Asset Classes 1 & 2.* As you can see, *Asset Class #1* and *Asset Class #2* are negatively correlated to each other meaning when one *Asset Class* is going up the other *Asset Class* is going down. These two *Asset Classes* are classified as non-correlated because they behave opposite to each other. When one is going up, the other one is going down.

The ups and downs of each *Asset Class* are the volatility of the *Asset Class* because each *Asset Class* moves opposite to each other their combined returns are smoothed out, which is represented by the centerline of the following chart.

Non-correlated Asset Classes smooth out your investment returns

Let's look at an example. Having these *Asset Classes* in your portfolio allows for rebalancing as well.

Let's use this example of buying 50% equities and 50% bonds.

Pretty soon, the markets will move, and you may have 60% equities and 40% bonds.

Does this make your portfolio more, or less risky?

Answer: Your portfolio would be riskier. If you leave it alone, the markets will eventually bring your portfolio back into line. However, you have missed an excellent opportunity.

Do you remember the buy low, sell high strategy? One way to take the emotion out of that decision and make systematic decisions is to use rebalancing.

Having a portfolio that you know is out of whack, and that one *Asset Class* has outperformed the other, forces you to systematically sell high and buy low by selling 10% of the equities to purchase 10% of the bonds to bring the portfolio back into balance.

In Summary

The future of asset management and the speed at which change is happening is absolutely astounding.

Any investor looking to preserve their wealth and even increase it in the next 10 to 20 years is advised to discuss *Alternative Asset Classes* with their *Wealth Advisor*.

By adding non-correlating *Asset Classes*, your portfolio would be positioned to grow to its maximum potential with significantly less risk.

Caveat Emptor:

No one; Investment Advisors, Wealth Advisors, nor Portfolio Managers can or should guarantee investment returns!

So, there you have them

The **7 KEY QUESTIONS** every financial advisor should be able to **ANSWER** to to protect yourself from **The Coming Financial Storm.**

Another big question.

A big question that always comes up when evaluating investments and investment opportunities is "What about my home as a retirement asset?"

In the next chapter, I will discuss this in detail.

My conclusions may surprise you.

CHAPTER 9

IS YOUR HOME
A GOOD RETIREMENT ASSET?

Since the tech bubble meltdown almost two decades ago, central banks, as well as international bankers, have been playing fast and loose with national and international monetary policy.

In simple terms, reducing interest rates on bank loans of all kinds to increase borrowing, had two immediate results:

1. businesses borrowed money to purchase assets and company shares,

2. banks increased their lending portfolios and offered incentives to mortgage borrowers – mostly in terms of lower interest rates.

LOW RATES FUEL HOUSING

CANADIAN REAL ESTATE ASSOCIATION HOUSING PRICE
IN THOUSANDS OF DOLLARS
Left scale ——

GOVERNMENT OF CANADA FIVE-YEAR BOND
YIELD CURVE IN PER CENT
—— Right scale

SOURCE: TRIVEST WEALTH COUNSEL

NATIONAL POST

Source: Greater Fool Authored by Garth Turner The Troubled Future of Real Estate[53]

As mortgage rates dropped, house prices increased (see graph above). More money was available to buy homes, and so the value of homes increased astronomically.

Who would have thought that?

The following graph below clearly shows the relationship between debt growth, house price increases, and wages.

[53] "In Disguise." *Greater Fool Authored by Garth Turner The Troubled Future of Real Estate RSS*, https://www.greaterfool.ca/2016/12/29/in-disguise/.

Growth in Canadian house prices, household debt and after-tax income
Index: 2000 = 100
Sources: Teranet-National Bank National Composite House Price (11 city) Index™, Statistics Canada, Bank for International Settlements,
The MacBeth Group - February 2017

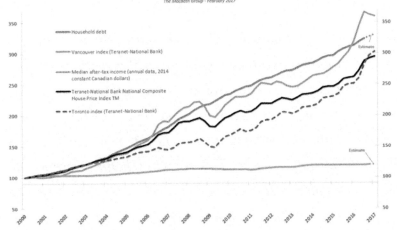

Source: Hilliard MacBeth, "Drop the Pretense"

"Much of this debt growth would have been impossible without the housing bubble. And the corollary is true: The housing price bubble couldn't have grown so large without unprecedented growth in household debt.

Household debt has more than tripled since 2000, with the index starting at 100 and now above 300. Household debt is even more stretched in the key housing markets of Toronto and Vancouver."[54]

As you can clearly see, this increase in house prices was almost completely fueled by an increase of household debt as household income barely increased during the time illustrated in the graph.

[54] Team, MacBeth. "Drop the Pretense." *Welcome - Digital Agent*, 17 Feb. 2017, https://web.richardsongmp.com/macbeth.macleod/blog/1395012-Drop-the-pretense.

The Collateral Effect

"The withdrawal of home equity tells us a lot, but today we're focusing on the collateral effect. This is when people extract home equity to spend, as home prices rise. What's the point of being a multi-millionaire bungalow owner, if you can't have a few toys – right? This spending helps to propel the economy. It's a twofer – home prices rise, and the economy gets a boost. Score!

BoC researchers warn this is a problem if the collateral effect contributes meaningfully. If home prices fall, the equity-based spending disappears. Combine that with slower sales, which leads to lower spin-off economic activity. A decline in home prices is no longer just a hit to paper-based wealth. It has a significant impact on the general economy and employment."[55]

[55] Punwasi, Stephen, Co-Founder, Better Dwelling. "Bank of Canada: Canadian Homeowners Have Extracted Hundreds of Billions In Equity." *Better Dwelling*, 24 Sept. 2019, https://betterdwelling.com/bank-of-canada-canadian-homeowners-have-extracted-hundreds-of-billions-in-equity/.

Seriously, It's A Lot Of Home Equity Extracted

"The equity extraction problem is much larger than is currently discussed. National property values increased $333 billion in 2015, the most recent StatCan estimate. That same year, a whopping $82.9 billion in home equity was extracted. The equivalent of one-quarter of the increase in property values was extracted." (ibid)

"The interesting thing is how home value estimates are created, in contrast to debt values. Home values are based on a projection, inferred by what marginal buyers have been paying. If you understand how marginal buyers impact prices, you understand how quickly values move in either direction. Debt, on the other hand, is based on an actual amount owing, not inferred. This setup is similar to the one found in the US, pre-Great Recession.

*Post-Great Recession, not all markets give up all gains made during the price run. **However, many homeowners didn't see their net-worth improve due to equity extraction**."* (ibid)

Housing Market Background

In the years leading up to the peak of the Canadian housing bubble in the spring of 2017, homeowners in the Greater Toronto and Greater Vancouver regions, saw their home prices rise on a weekly basis.

Some homeowners in BC, seeing their home values increase, sold, took their massive gains, and left Vancouver for regions that had not yet seen these massive home value increases. Selling their mortgage-free home for a million dollars, meant they could buy in the Fraser Valley, Kelowna and points east, be mortgage-free and have hundreds of thousands of dollars in the bank or in investments to fund their lifestyle.

Homeowners who sold before June 2017 were home free.

Greater Toronto saw similar increases, but not quite at the same level of BC.

The Real Estate Boards in Ontario and BC, seeing dollar signs everywhere as people bought and sold, continued to promote the increasing value of homes. The result was a mania to purchase a home before the prices went up and they couldn't afford a home. **FOMO, Fear Of Missing Out** set in, causing panic buying, especially among millenials at any price as long as they qualified.

As single-family home values rose into the millions, condo developers saw an opportunity to build towers of condos for all those people who couldn't afford those million-dollar homes, but still wanted to buy real estate.

In Ontario and BC, we saw hundreds of proposed condo towers promote presale opportunities where one could buy a condo that would be built in two to three years.

Who would buy under those circumstances?

People who thought prices would go up forever.

They wanted a piece of the real estate bonanza. Whether they bought for themselves or as an investment opportunity, this mania continued to drive real estate values to the moon.

As this real estate bubble grew, boomer homeowners were faced with a dilemma.

They owned a single-family home that had increased in value astronomically. If they sold, they were set for life.

However, their children were left out in the cold. There was little hope for them to buy expensive homes or condos with little or no money for down payments.

House ownership dreams were increasing, and yet financial capabilities were decreasing.

What could be done?

Enter the *Bank of Mom*. Mom, bless her soul, wanted Johnny and Mary and her grandbabies, to have the same home security she had.

After prevailing upon her hubby repeatedly, they remortgaged their home or took out a Home Equity Line of Credit (HELOC) to provide junior or juniorette with a down payment to an overpriced townhouse or condo, *putting their own retirement at risk.*

The result: increased demand, so townhouse and condo prices continued to rise.

I saw this happen first hand as a contractor client of mine; five years from retirement saw his contract business dry up as his former clients (national firms) moved their business renovations internally.

The client had a retirement portfolio with me of approximately $1,000,000 and a home worth just over $900,000 with a $600,000 mortgage. Although unable to find work, the client maintained the same lifestyle as if he was still working, against my advice. He thought new business would be just around the corner, so he did not cut back.

In the meantime, house prices were surging. They were concerned that their three children would be priced out of the market, so they raided their RRSPs to raise the down payments for each of their three children. They were convinced that this was a great investment to help each of their children purchase a townhome, as real estate at the time was growing at a rate greater than their portfolio was.

So, against my advice, they withdrew the money from their RRSPs to fund their children's down payments over a two-year period. After paying the taxes, their RRSPs were reduced to approximately 50% of their original value.

Their lifestyle expenditures over the next five years reduced their RRSP's to zero, and so they were forced to tap into their home equity line of credit (HELOC). After seven years of being my clients, they were no longer my clients, had a house valued at over $1,200,000 with an $800,000 mortgage.

The last time I met with them, they had their house listed for sale, they were having a difficult time selling the house getting deeper into debt each month the house was on the market. Their plan was to sell the house to take whatever equity was left and move in with one of their children.

The remainder of their retirement assets are tied up as a down payment in the three townhouses they helped their children purchase. The townhouses have since declined in value so much that most of their down payment would be lost if the townhouses sold at current market prices after real estate commissions.

So? What does the home market landscape look like?

Thousands of boomers with single-family homes valued in the $1,000,000s. Afraid to sell because they may not be able to buy another home.

Why not rent? Renting has a whole series of disadvantages – the biggest being the lack of prestige of being a homeowner.

And what has happened to the best-laid plans of mice and men that one's home is the best retirement plan?

Three problems exist for those who view their home as a retirement plan:

1. Depending on the market, selling a home can be a complicated and time-consuming process, which may take weeks and sometimes months.
2. What happens if the housing market tanks?
3. What happens when you have used much of your equity for helping your children buy a home, or, squandered your equity on personal trips, toys, and trinkets.

What do others say?

Here's the problem with relying on your home as a retirement plan according to Garth Turner, former Conservative Minister of National Revenue of Canada:

*"**First**, real estate lust has had terrible consequences. Sure, some people in some places bought
low and have made a pile of dough. Most have not.
Instead, they've saved little and borrowed much.
**Theirs is a one-asset strategy and, sadly, houses
don't pay you a pension.**
Second, interest rates are so low nobody can retire
on GIC income. This won't change. Those who fear
investing, or don't know how may suffer as a result.
Third, our culture of savings has been shot. It's
astonishing how we've changed. A generation ago,
people routinely saved 10-15% of what they earned.
The average over the previous decade was 7%. Now
it's collapsed. It's dead. After inflation, our national
savings rate is negative. Hard to overstate this – we
have the worst rate in 60 years at just 0.7% of income
(inflation is 2%). That's 63% below the level of just a
year ago. In other words, in the first quarter of this
year, we saved (on average) just twenty bucks per
person per month. Ouch.
Fourth, people grossly underestimate the pile
they'll need. Life is long. People retiring at 65
require enough to last a quarter-century.
Those FIRE weirdos who seek to stop working at
age 40 (to do what?) need a pile so big it'll last 50
years. Good luck with that."*

Fifth, public pogey won't save you. At least if you dislike poverty. And corporate pensions are disappearing or being turned into crappy insurance-company, mutual-fund puddles. CPP and OAS? The average collected is $679 a month. The old-age thing is $607. Combined, that's only $15,400 a year. For a couple, it would equal less than $31,000 – and yet StatsCan says the average amount spent by retired households is $61,000.[56]

What does History Tell Us About the Housing Market?

The following chart is a cautionary tale.

In the late 1970s, the Japanese experienced the beginning of a massive real estate bubble, which peaked in 1991.

The Japanese believed their real estate prices would go up forever. The third quarter of 1991 was the beginning of a 25-year slide. By 2016, the prices levelled off and have only now begun a slow increase.

The same trend happened in the US between 1999 and 2008. In 2006 - 2007 as the US loosened it's mortgage lending rules

[56] "What Are We Thinking?" Greater Fool Authored by Garth Turner The Troubled Future of Real Estate RSS, https://www.greaterfool.ca/2019/08/29/what-are-we-thinking/.

and handed out mortgages to anyone who could fog a mirror, the public believed that home prices would go up forever. Alas, that hope was dashed with the financial crisis of 2008. Only recently have US home prices begun their upward trend.

Now, look at Canada.

Have a look at what has happened to home prices.

Index of real house prices in
Canada, the U.S. and Japan
100 = 2005

What if you were the unfortunate homeowner who purchased their home in 1980 at peak 1980's prices? The early 1980s saw massive interest rate increases (up to 22% in some cases), which caused home prices to fall.

[57]"Canada's Housing Market Looks A Lot Like The U.S. Did In 2006." *MACLEAN'S* N.p., n.d. Web. 02 Aug. 2019 https://www.macleans.ca/economy/economicanalysis/canadas-housing-market-looks-a-

The straight horizontal line starting from the peak of the Canadian house prices in 1980 illustrates that you would have to wait until 1990 to see your home reach 1980's prices, after adjusting for inflation.

If you did not sell in 1990, you would have had to wait until 2003 for your house to finally be worth more than when you bought it in 1980 after adjusting for inflation.

In other words, you would have held onto your house paying interest on your mortgage, property taxes, and maintenance on your house. If you factor the cost of holding onto your house, you were still underwater.

From the previous chart, (which by the way ends in 2016), can you see why Canadians also believed that Canadian real estate prices could go up forever as well?

I believe we will suffer a fate similar to the Japanese and Americans.

We were led to believe that house prices always go up, especially in Canada.

The graph below shows that Canada has now surpassed Japan's peak house prices in 2017 and is now correcting.

Canada Vs. Other G7 Real Estate Prices

Inflation adjusted index of G7 real estate prices.

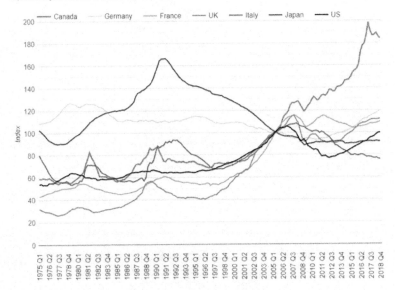

Source: US Federal Reserve, Better Dwelling.[58]

The chart on the next page is from Brian Ripley's Canadian Housing Price Charts website and his Plunge-o-meter page at http://www.chpc.biz/plunge-o-meter.html.

---

[58] Wong, Daniel , Contributing Editor. "Canadian Real Estate Prices Down 7% From Peak, But Still 52% Above G7 Peers." *Better Dwelling*, 10 Apr. 2019, https:/ /betterdwelling.com/canadian-real-estate-prices-down-7-from-peak-but-still-52-above-g7-peers/.

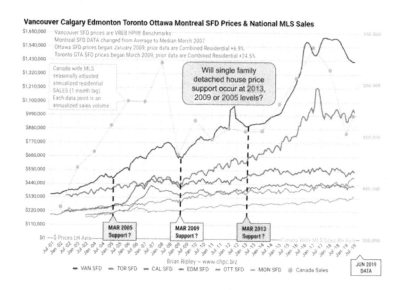

Source: Canadian Housing Price Charts & Plunge-O-Meter[59]

The chart above covers Vancouver, Calgary, Edmonton, Toronto, Ottawa, and Montreal Single Family Dwelling (SFD) prices over an eighteen-year period from July 2001 to July 2019.

The solid top line represents the Vancouver MLS sales figures. This chart shows the small peaks in July 2008 and March 2012. July 2016 saw a massive increase to over a million dollars per house and a market peak in July 2017.

---

[59] "Plunge-o-meter At Brian Ripley's Canadian Housing Price Charts - *Chpc.biz.*" N.p., n.d. Web. 01 Aug. 2019 http://www.chpc.biz/plunge-o-meter.html.

Since July 2018, sales prices have started to drop significantly.

What caused this drop-in prices?

In BC, we had some significant government intervention. The BC government, under the NDP, introduced Bill 28 providing for a 15% foreign buyers tax in August 2016.

BNN, Business News Network wrote that: "Home sales dropped 40% by October 2016.

In 2018, the Foreign Buyer's Tax was extended to the Fraser Valley, the Capital Region, Nanaimo, and Central Okanagan Regional Districts, at 20%.[60]

Vancouver prices bottomed in June 2017 and started to rise. Then the City of Vancouver imposed a Speculation and Vacancy Tax (SVT) in January of 2018 and home prices started to drop again and continue to drop.

The following is another chart that shows how B.C. housing prices changed in response to the announcement of foreign buyers and speculation taxes.

[60] "Bill 28 (British Columbia) - *Wikipedia*." N.p., n.d. Web. 01 Aug. 2019 https://en.wikipedia.org/wiki/Bill_28_(British_Columbia).

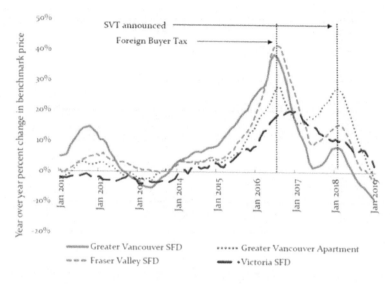

Source: CREA/ Teranet - Chart shows how B.C. housing prices changed in response to the announcement of the foreign buyers and speculation taxes. (SFU social policy specialist Josh Gordon).[61]

In his April 2nd, 2019 blog post titled "*The Spiral*" Garth Turner writes:

> "*That was conjecture about Vancouver's real estate disaster in March. Now we have the facts. Not since people were humming the latest Bananarama tune have things sucked this much. Sales are collapsing. Prices are falling. Equity's evaporating. And where are the buyers everyone thought would descend to snap up bargains once the street value of a detached house plunged by double digits? Yup. Gone. Because nobody pounces in a declining market – figuring things will get worse. Good bet.*

[61] "Bill 28 (British Columbia) - *Wikipedia*." N.p., n.d. Web. 01 Aug. 2019 https://en.wikipedia.org/wiki/Bill_28_(British_Columbia).

Prices? Down she goes. The benchmark Franken-number is off almost 8% in a year. Detached have fallen 11% and condos about 6%. Probably just a start, since the goal of politicians in BC is to destroy home equity and artificially depress the market. To do that they have enacted the 20% foreign buyer's tax, the anti-Alberta speculation tax, the eat-the-rich empty houses tax plus the special property tax on wealthy owners. This is atop the stress test which has reduced the credit by a fifth, and hood-busting zoning changes as well as pro-tenant legislation driving off landlords."[62]

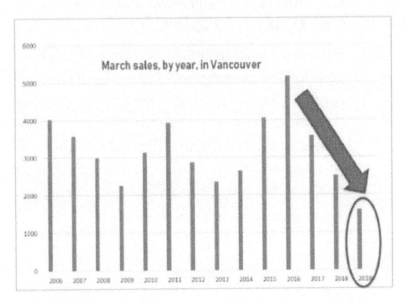

Source: The Spiral — Greater Fool – Authored by Garth Turner – The Troubled Future of Real Estate

[62]"The Spiral — *Greater Fool – Authored by Garth Turner - The Troubled Future of Real Estate* N.p., n.d. Web. 26 Jul. 2019 https://www.greaterfool.ca/2019/04/02/the-spiral/

Turner continues in an article at ***HoweStreet.com***:

"The culprit? "Demand-side taxes," he says. The disincentives to buy in the Lower Mainland are now legion. A speculation tax. An empty-houses (or under-utilized) tax. Higher property tax on expensive homes. The foreign buyer tax. And the promise of more to come. Then, of course, there's the stress test. A perfect governmental storm concocted by politicians who can't resist trying to screw with market forces. "Something has to give," Sullivan says, as BCers deal with higher taxes and less wealth. (By the way, locals have more of their net worth in their homes than anywhere else in Canada, says our central bank.)

Meanwhile, a Reuters poll of economists finds an expectation Van prices will fall further throughout 2019. "The major risk right now is with the overextended consumer," says Peter Norman, chief economist at Altus Group. "With interest rates now levelled off, this risk is sidelined, but there continues to be stress in terms of the consumer's ability to take on increased spending."[63]

---

[63] "Too Human – *Howestreet.*" N.p., n.d. Web. 26 Jul. 2019 https://www.howestreet.com/2019/05/21/too-human/.

HOUSING PRICES PLUNGE ACROSS METRO VANCOUVER

Change in the median sales prices of housing in select markets between 2018 and 2019. Values were calculated by taking the median sales prices from January to April of each year.

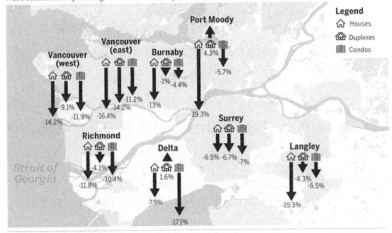

SOURCE: REBGV, FVRB, FREEPIK (ICONS)   N. GRIFFITHS / POSTMEDIA NEWS

Source: Postmedia News graphic, REBGV statistics

According to the July 2019, issue of ***Better Dwelling***, British Columbia has the fastest cooling real estate market in Canada. With cooling markets comes further price reductions with no end in sight.

"The fastest falling real estate markets were all located in British Columbia. Fraser Valley is the fastest falling with a Sales to Listing Ratio (SNLR) of 44.9% in June, down 17.4% from last year. Vancouver followed with a ratio of 38.9%, down 16.7% from last year. Victoria came in third with a ratio of 57.7%, down 8.8% from last year. British Columbian, real estate markets, have been leading the way lower for a few months now.

Vancouver real estate keeps getting colder, after an epic run for the history books. The SNLR fell to 38.9% in June, down 16.7% from the same month last year. The decline puts the ratio 39.0% below the ratio in June 2017.

Vancouver's real estate market is in buyer's market territory. Something quite a few people doubted could ever happen again. [64]

Residential property prices could fall by 40%

*"Residential property prices could drop by as much as **40% over the next five years**, led by declines in Toronto and Vancouver, according to David Madani, senior Canadian economist for **Capital Economics**."* [65]

If that wasn't bad enough, thousands of recent property buyers with high loan-to-value mortgages could be plunged deep into negative equity, Madani warned.

*"I see a **correction of between 20 to 40 percent** in the Canadian housing market – over five years,"* Madani said in an interview this week.

[64] Last, Kaitlin. Contributing Editor. "B.C. Is Home To The Fastest Cooling Real Estate Markets In Canada." *Better Dwelling*, 23 July 2019, https://betterdwelling.com/b-c-is-home-to-the-fastest-cooling-real-estate-markets-in-canada/.

[65] "Residential Property Prices Could Fall By 40% - *Which Mortgage*" N.p., n.d. Web. 12 Aug. 2019 https://www.whichmortgage.ca/article/residential-property-prices-could-fall-by-40-226911.aspx

He noted that Vancouver and Toronto's housing markets are trapped in a speculation-fuelled bubble that appears to be on the verge of popping, which would instigate a major correction.

In a speculative housing bubble, once prices stop going up, the whole reason for speculating in the market disappears," he said."[(ibid)]

Lessons from 380 years of Dutch house price data

*"As the chart below illustrates, over a 380-year period, the real (**i.e., inflation-adjusted**) house prices have only doubled, which corresponds to an annual average price increase of something like 0.1%. And that's with a starting point just at the start of the Dutch golden age. With a different starting point, one could just as well get a 0% or even negative annual price change.*

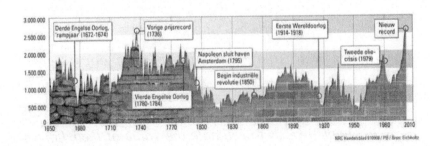

Source: Martin. "A Very Long View on House Prices." *Hotel Ivory*

So, the conclusion is that there are ups and downs, but that over time, prices roughly follow inflation. **To expect house prices to rise much faster than inflation every year over a 10- or 20-year period without reverting down again does not make much sense.** *"* [66]

Case-Shiller US Home Price Index

"Shiller notes that there is a strong perception across the globe that home prices are continuously increasing and that this kind of sentiment and paradigm may be fueling bubbles in real estate markets. He points to some psychological heuristics that may be responsible for creating this perception. He says that since homes are relatively infrequent purchases, people tend to remember the purchase price of a home from long ago and are surprised at the difference between then and now. However, most of the difference in the prices can be explained by inflation.

He also discusses how people consistently overestimate the appreciation in the value of their homes. The US Census, since 1940, has asked homeowners to estimate the value of their homes.

[66] Martin. "A Very Long View on House Prices." *Hotel Ivory*, 19 Nov. 2011, https://hotelivory.wordpress.com/2010/08/29/a-very-long-view-on-house-prices/

The home-owners' estimates reflect an appreciation of 2% per year in real terms, which is significantly more than the 0.7% actual increase over the same interval as reflected in Case–Shiller index.[67]

As the next graph below from *VisualizingEconomics* illustrates, US house prices have barely kept up with inflation since 1890.

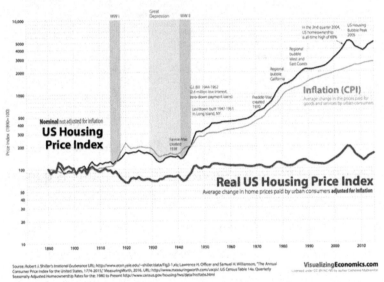

Source: VisualizingEconomics[68]

[67] "Case–Shiller Index." *Wikipedia*, Wikimedia Foundation, 7 June 2019, https://en.wikipedia.org/wiki/Case–Shiller_index
[68] "Log Scale - Blog." *Visualizing Economics*, http://visualizingeconomics.com/blog/tag/Log+scale

This next graph from *Advisor Perspectives* further illustrates that US house prices have barely kept up with inflation since 1950 and only outpaced inflation from 2000 on as a result of the housing bubble.

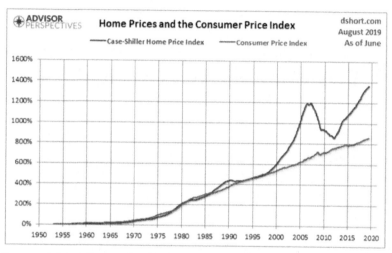

Source: Advisor Perspectives[69]

In a Maclean's article titled "*A chart to put Canadian Housing bubble in perspective,*" Robert Shiller is quoted:

"*Canada's success story is uncomfortably similar to the U.S. success story. It might be offensive to Canadians, but we're like two peas in a pod.*" [70]

[69] *Advisorperspectives.com*, https://www.advisorperspectives.com/dshort/updates/2019/08/27/s-p-case-shiller-home-price-index-inflation-adjusted-indexes-down-mom.
[70] Kirby, Jason. "A Chart to Put the Canadian Housing Bubble in Perspective." *Macleans.ca*, 14 Mar. 2014, https://www.macleans.ca/economy/realestateeconomy/a-canadian-housing-chart-that-puts-the-bubble-in-perspective

In the chart below, Robert Shiller splices 20 years of Canadian inflation-adjusted house price history onto his Case-Shiller US Home Price Index going back to 1890.

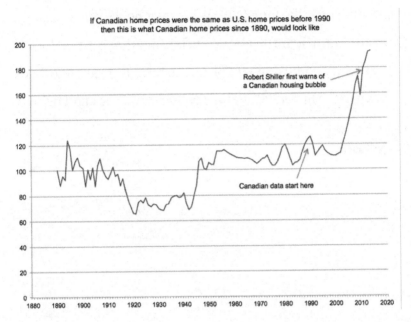

Source: Kirby, Jason. "A Chart to Put the Canadian Housing Bubble in Perspective." *Macleans.ca*

"It was an "experiment," he said. (it assumed Canadian prices behaved generally similar to U.S. prices before 1990, and the early Canadian data was based on a limited number of housing markets) the resulting chart served to show how unusual this housing boom has been in comparison to booms in the U.S. before 1990." [(ibid)]

As the four charts above illustrate, global house prices have barely averaged above inflation over the long term.

History has shown us that house prices basically mirror inflation over the long haul. Whenever house prices grow at a rate significantly above inflation, those prices must eventually come down to bring the long-time average back down to the historical average or "*mean*." (See chart below).

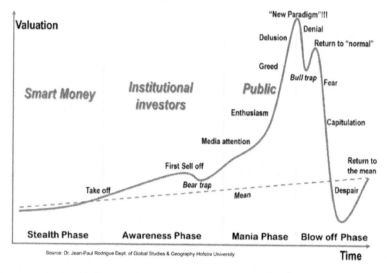

Source: *Anatomy of a Bubble*

"The above chart was formulated by Dr. Jean-Paul Rodrigue in 2006, in the middle of the developing US housing bubble. It illustrates the general pattern that most market bubbles tend to follow."[71]

[71] "Anatomy of a Bubble." *228Main*, 29 Dec. 2015, https://228main.com/2015/11/23/anatomy-of-a-bubble/

This graph clearly illustrates that all bubbles eventually crash and values average back to the long term average of inflation or *"Mean,"* the straight dotted line in this graph. The Canadian housing market is currently in the *"Denial"* stage illustrated on the chart above since peaking in 2017. As of August 2019, the Toronto and Vancouver real estate boards are celebrating a market recovery.

Prices are rising again. This is the *"Return to Normal"* phase of the bubble. This phase is sometimes called a *"Dead Cat Bounce."* Next, we will enter the *"Fear"* stage followed by the *"Capitulation"* stage and finally the *"Despair"* stage. This is how all bubbles end and how the *Canadian Housing Bubble* will eventually end. What we do not know is how quickly or how slowly this will happen.

Since the Canadian housing market has outperformed inflation significantly for the past 20 years, and it appears that we are entering the *"Return to Normal"* phase, house prices have a long way to come down before they match the long-term average of inflation.

On top of that, interest rates have reached rock bottom and can only go up from here. While there may not be interest rate pressure just yet, the long term outlook for interest rates is higher.

As the opening graph in this chapter illustrated, falling interest rates had a direct negative correlation to housing prices. Meaning that house prices increased in direct proportion to interest rates declining. Now that interest rates are set to rise, the exact opposite will happen. As interest rates begin to rise, house prices will drop in direct proportion to interest rates rising further, adding to the downward pressure on house prices for the next decade or two or three, much like Japan has experienced.

Jeremy Grantham, of GMO, a Boston-based money management firm, reminds us that all bubbles burst.

> *"His staff studied 28 different bubbles, from stocks to real estate, and found that, without exception, all bubbles underwent "**Reversion To The Mean**." Grantham said, "all 28 major bubbles ... eventually retreated all the way back to the original trend, the trend that had existed prior to each bubble, a very tough standard indeed."*
> *Grantham's assertion that all prices revert back to the trend line, as happened in the U.S. from 2006 to 2010, means a **price drop of 40% or more** in Canada would be comparatively worse than the U.S. correction because Canada's bubble is bigger. But the second reason, an excess of debt, is even more compelling."[72]*

[72] MacBeth, Hilliard. "The Canadian Housing Bubble Revisited." *Welcome - Digital Agent*, 8 Jan. 2016, https://web.richardsongmp.com/macbeth.macleod/blog/775609-The-Canadian-housing-bubble-revisited

Political Interference

As I write this, we are in the middle of a federal election campaign. In an effort to attract the precious millennial vote, politicians are scrambling over each other to offer incentives to make housing affordable. This effort may create a temporary reprieve to the correction that has been underway since 2017, but it will not stop the inevitable.

In his September 27th, 2019 blog post titled "*The Bribes*" Garth Turner writes:

> "*In the last few days, for example, the governing party says it will hand out $40,000 interest-free loans for house upgrades. That comes atop the enhanced down payment/RRSP limit, the shared-equity mortgage and a new tax on non-maple buyers. The Tories have tried to keep up with a return to 30-year mortgages, a gutted stress test and retrofit cash.*
>
> *Maybe it's time we paleos just rolled over and accepted the fact nobody under 40 cares about fiscal sustainability, ethical leadership or less government. Federal deficits and national debt are remote, icy concepts. The big issues of demographics, pensions and productivity are pffft.*

Instead, younger leaders catering to younger votes focus on wants and desires. At the top of the list, weirdly, is property.

So, no wonder we're seeing the kind of crap reporting that's flooded social media lately. It reinforces the meme that moisters are screwed, implying Boomers are the screwees. A great example comes from the online real estate portal Zoocasa where the kids decided to find out how long it would take houseless Millennials to afford the average home in major cities. The conclusion was shocking – in Vancouver, the typical household would need 52 years. Toronto was a bargain. Only 32 years.

The fake news even came with a snappy chart... "[73]

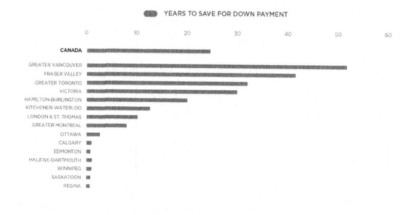

Source: The Bribes."*Greater Fool Authored by Garth Turner The Troubled Future of Real* Estate RSS https://www.greaterfool.ca/2019/09/27/the-bribes/(ibid)

[73] "The Bribes." *Greater Fool Authored by Garth Turner The Troubled Future of Real Estate RSS*, https://www.greaterfool.ca/2019/09/27/the-bribes/.

"Why is this the wrong data on which to base national housing policies? Simple. In demand markets where average prices are seven figures, nobody should expect to jump from no real estate at all to a detached house with three bedrooms and shiny taps. The notion of a 'property ladder' has even more validity in big cities where single-family homes are in limited supply. Families buying mid-priced real estate are usually trading up based on equity earned by selling cheaper properties." (ibid)

Summary

There you have a brief explanation of the ups and downs of residential real estate. It's not a pretty picture, and no one knows how far down it will go this time.

Many boomers have put their hopes into being able to sell their homes for significantly more than they paid for it many years ago to finance their retirement.

Many put their net worth into a single, leveraged asset whose value is often determined by governments, government monetary policy, and general economic conditions.

Lower Mainland homeowners who sold before June 2017 made out very well.

Recently, sales numbers have dropped, and listings have spiralled upwards, but prices have not yet dropped precipitously.

Many homeowners may be living in the *Land of Hope*, where they **HOPE** to sell their home for 2017 prices. As a result, they are not dropping asking prices. How long these homeowners can live with this belief is anyone's guess.

Final Thoughts:

Don't get me wrong; I am not negative on real estate, as I have illustrated in Chapter 8. Real estate is an important *Alternative Asset Class* in a well-diversified portfolio.

What I am negative on is using your home as your retirement plan, as many boomers have done over the past 20 years.

Your home is a lifestyle choice, *not your retirement plan*.

There are ways to invest in *Real Estate* that are not dependent on inflation and capital appreciation, where the price you pay for *Real Estate* is based on the positive cash flow generated by the *Real Estate* investment instead of *hysteria*. This would include:

1. Newly constructed in-fill or fully renovated rental apartments in urban centers that appeal to millennials in regions of the country that are not overvalued and subject to rent controls;

2. Commercial property and office buildings that cater to the medical profession;

3. Retirement and nursing homes that benefit from the aging boomer population.

The discussion on *Investment-Grade Real Estate* is beyond the scope of this book and will be the topic of my next book.

If you have been relying on your home as your retirement plan, now is the time to consider downsizing.

This will allow you to extract the excess equity from your current home to secure your retirement before the market winds change.

As more and more boomers enter retirement and look at cashing out of their home and putting money into retirement, it will soon become difficult to sell your home when YOU need the money for your retirement.

In the beginning, on page 20, I asked three more questions about advisors that often arise.

a. What type of advisor should I choose?

b. What can I expect in terms of fees?

c. What comprehensive services should my advisor be offering?

I will elaborate on these three additional questions in the next chapter.

CHAPTER 10

WHAT TYPE OF ADVISOR SHOULD I CHOOSE?

Why is this important? Two Main Reasons:

REASON #1

If you hire or are working with a financial advisor who does not take a holistic approach to managing your wealth, you may be working with an advisor who does not see the big financial picture in your life and only will advise within their core competency.

They may shy away from giving you advice or directing you to someone who can give you advice on other areas of your financial life critically important to your financial well-being.

REASON #2

Families may be getting incomplete advice.

If you **HIRE** or are working with an advisor who does not or cannot offer an integrated approach to managing your wealth, you will need to work with additional advisors to get a complete picture of your overall wealth.

Coordinating the advice from multiple advisors can be a challenge.

When you work with multiple advisors to provide advice on the various aspects of your financial life, you will find that they may not necessarily communicate with each other to get a full understanding of your overall investment strategy and financial goals.

As a result, they may offer conflicting and sometimes incomplete investment, tax, trust, business succession, and estate planning advice.

You may be making financial decisions that happen in isolation of your overall investment objectives and financial needs.

The result is a collection of investments that are **fragmented, expensive, not very tax-efficient, and not doing as well as you expected.**

Aren't All Financial Advisors the Same?

A wide range of differences exists between the expertise and services offered by the various types of financial advisors.

Not knowing what these differences are and hiring the wrong financial advisor can be harmful to your financial health. A financial advisor is a professional who renders financial services to clients. The terms such as financial advisor and financial specialist may be general terms or job titles used by investment professionals and do not denote any specific designations.

When evaluating investment advisors, selecting the advisor with the lowest fee possible may not always be the most prudent decision.

A *"Wealth Advisor"* or financial planner offering the services of **Portfolio Manager** can offer a full range of services for the same fee you may already be paying your stockbroker or mutual fund advisor.

When the fees charged are embedded (hidden), as they are in many mutual funds, the investor often mistakenly believes the service is free.

When the fee is charged separately or is disclosed, and the investor only receives investment advice, this advice becomes a commodity.

As a result, the only difference between advisors is the size of the advisors' fee.

The best way to evaluate advisors is by asking the seven questions above.

CHAPTER 11

WHAT CAN I EXPECT IN TERMS OF FEES?

Advisors are paid for their services in three ways:

1. Commissions;
2. Fee-based – Combination of commission and fee-only;
3. Fee-only.

1. Stockbrokers and mutual fund salespeople make money when they sell a stock or a fund.

- Stockbrokers receive a transaction fee or a flat fee for each stock or bond they put into your account. Fees may be transparent and are non-tax deductible.

- The fees for mutual funds are called loads and are charged:

    * as a front-load of up to 5% when your advisor buys a fund; or

    * as a *Deferred Sales Charge* (**DSC**) of up to 5.5% when your advisor sells a fund (the full commission is charged if sold in the first year and declines every year thereafter to $0, typically after seven years); or

    * on an annual flat fee basis of up to 3% per year based on *Assets Under Management* (**AUM**). Fees may not be fully transparent as the underlying mutual fund **MER** in fee-based accounts may not be fully disclosed.

    Mutual fund fees may be partially transparent and are not tax-deductible.

2. Fee-based advisors may receive both fees and commissions. They will charge fees based on *Assets Under Management* (**AUM**) for their financial/investment planning services and receive commissions for the products they recommend as well.

Total management fees can thus range from 1.25% to as high as 3.5% when you combine both investment advisor fees and mutual fund manager fees inside their fee-based accounts.

Advisor fees may be partially transparent and are usually not tax-deductible.

3. Fee-only advisors are paid directly by their clients and do not receive commissions or fees based on *Assets Under Management*. This fee can be a flat retainer fee or an hourly rate. The hourly or retainer fee can vary widely based on advisor experience and complexity of a client's financial affairs and can be very expensive. These fees are fully transparent and tax-deductible.

Fee Transparency

The Canadian Securities Administration under the new Client Relationship Model (CRM2) had sought to ban *Deferred Sales Charge* (**DSC**) fees due to their lack of disclosure issues. The Mutual Fund Industry fought back and won a partial victory.

Under the new regulations, mutual fund companies can continue to offer mutual funds with DSC fees. In return, they have agreed to provide better disclosure of fees. This decision is a compromise at best for the investor.

"CRM2 is a regulatory change by the Canadian Securities Administrator (CSA) and only applies to organizations that are regulated by the CSA. Segregated Funds are excluded from CRM2 reporting requirements. Since the investor must purchase segregated fund positions from an insurance agent, (who are not subject to CSA regulations) acting for an insurance company, all trades in segregated funds must take place outside of the CRM2 regulatory arena and, as a result, the requirement to provide disclosure of charges and performance does not apply to trades in segregated funds." [74]

---

[74]"Investing for me - Understand the Client Relationship Model Phase 2" Investing for Me the Science of Investing. N.p., n.d. Web. 12 Jul. 2019 https://www.investingforme.com/-understand-the-client-relationship-model-phase-2-crm2

Portfolio Managers

Portfolio Managers charge a percentage of the investments they manage. This fee is transparent and generally much less than retail management fees and distribution costs, which are often embedded as a cost of doing business.

Portfolio Manager fees are fully tax-deductible on non-registered investment accounts.

> *"It's important to note that your money must reside at a custodian financial institution for an extra layer of protection and safety, and there is usually a small additional fee for this service.*
>
> *Fees are fully transparent on client statements and typically go down as a percentage of your portfolio as your assets grow.*
>
> *Fees are not commission based on the dollar volume of buying or selling investments and are significantly lower than typical mutual fund fees."*[75]

[75]"What Is A Portfolio Manager? - Pmac." Portfolio Management Association of Canada. N.p., n.d. Web. 12 Jul. 2019 https://pmac.org/nav-investor-info/selection-checklist/.

Some people ask, "Why should I pay you for the services my commission advisor does for free?" They believe, incorrectly, that commission advisors are not being paid by the client.

Recall that the advisor is indeed being compensated either by commission or transaction fee for brokers or by having the mutual fund company deduct the fee from the investments or by charging a fee directly.

One important factor to consider is that for the same fee (or commission) that you pay a stockbroker or mutual fund representative to buy and sell stocks and funds, you can receive comprehensive, investment and wealth planning from a full-service Wealth Advisor.

The fee you pay, either embedded or visible, should be based on the value you receive. If the advice given is just pure investment advice, then the fee should be lower.

If the advice includes an Investment Policy Statement (IPS), financial planning, retirement planning, estate planning, Business or Farm Succession Planning, tax planning and integrated wealth management, the fee should reflect the additional value from the services provided.

A fee-based or fee-only advisor will have access to a wide range of additional services that can add significant value. The fee they charge should reflect the level of services they provide and the value you receive from these services.

The Bottom Line?

1. When evaluating investment advisors, selecting the advisor with the lowest fee may not always be the most prudent decision.

2. To get full value for the fees you are paying, you should hire a *Wealth Advisor* or financial planner who offers or has access to fully integrated investment and wealth management services.

3. *Wealth Advisors* who offer, or have access to, an investment management team will have a disciplined asset allocation process designed specifically for your unique needs.

4. Some *Wealth Advisors* offer or have access to private money managers that focus on maximizing your after-tax rate of return. Taxes are probably one of the largest expenditures that you will make over your lifetime.

Check your investment management fees. If you are already paying the standard embedded mutual fund management fee between 2% – 2.75% and are only getting investment advice, you should ask your advisor if they can offer integrated wealth management services.

If your advisor is unable to offer these services, you may want to consider the services of a *Wealth Advisor* or financial planner who offers or has access to integrated wealth management services.

In many cases, your overall cost for investment management and wealth planning advice is available to you for the same fee or even less than what you may already be paying your current financial advisor for just their investment advice alone!

CHAPTER 12

WHAT COMPREHENSIVE SERVICES SHOULD MY ADVISOR BE OFFERING?

What happens when individuals forgo advice and think they can do it on their own? They may often find themselves ill-prepared for some of the most important financial and life-changing decisions they will encounter in their lifetimes.

Here are three examples of how *Wealth Advisors* are valuable allies in the fight to reduce taxes and how to deal with conflicting advice from various advisors.

Example 1

As they neared retirement, a couple wanted to divest their interest in a business. The company balance sheet had some anomalies, and they agreed to a review by a tax lawyer and an accountant.

Canadian shareholders are entitled to a one-time $866,912 lifetime capital gains exemption in 2019 if their company qualifies as a *Qualified Small Business Corporation* (**QSBC**). The criteria for businesses are rigorous, and if they are unable to meet the criteria, the tax implications are serious.

The accountant mentioned the company was looking at a tax liability of $250,000 for failing to meet the criteria.

The accountant also discovered that the couple's partners owned a holding company with a $450,000 insurance policy on each of the partners, with the partners being direct beneficiaries of the policies. Since the policies were owned by the company and the premiums were paid by the company these policies posed a significant tax liability. Should either of the insured die, the insured's estate would receive the proceeds, and the proceeds would be taxable to the deceased's estate. The potential tax liability was approximately $220,000 for each partner.

To rectify this potential tax liability, the company was

named the beneficiary rather than either partner. Should a partner die, the insurance proceeds would then be received by the company tax-free and be paid out as a dividend to the surviving shareholder tax-free through the corporation's capital dividend account.

Soon after the changes one of the partners passed away, and the spouse received the full $450,000 insurance proceeds tax-free, saving her almost $220,000 in taxes.

The Lifetime Capital Gains exemption and the insurance policy restructuring meant total tax savings of $470,000.

Example 2

For over 15 years, a businessman resisted undertaking a detailed financial plan and financial check-up. Finally, when he took ill, he relented and provided all his financial documents (personal and business).

I had a tax lawyer review the legal documents. The lawyer noted the client was bequeathing his wife $500,000 and a life interest in the family home in his will as well as an additional $500,000 from a trust. She would receive a total of $1,000,000 and a life interest in the family home.

In the discussion, the client indicated his wife was to receive the home and only $500,000. The misunderstanding arose when a second, different lawyer set up an Alter-Ego

Trust at the request of the accountant to protect the client's personal assets from his estate. This included a provision for an additional $500,000 from the trust as well.

A simple correction resolved this misunderstanding, and the beneficiary once again stood to receive a life interest in the home and only $500,000.

This is an example of how important it is to have competent professionals available to assess your complete financial picture.

It's true that not all financial plans are this complex, but having access to a team that can deliver answers to complex problems is a welcome change.

Example 3

A retired farm couple owned a holding company that held the proceeds from the sale of their farm quota. By claiming their personal lifetime capital gains exemptions, they were able to extract capital out of their holding company. However, they still had approximately $550,000 remaining in their holding company.

Their children had no interest in taking over the farm, so the money could not be rolled over to their children. The couple had significant assets outside of their holding company, so there was no need to withdraw money from the holding company to maintain their lifestyle.

My clients wanted to wind down the holding company as it was a dead asset as far as they were concerned and a potentially significant tax liability to their children.

With a life expectancy of over 15 years, the couple saw that their assets in the holding company would easily grow to over $1,000,000.

Years ago, the farm couple had purchased a $500,000 joint last-to-die insurance policy as an estate planning tool to reduce personal taxes on their death. Upon reviewing their current tax situation and seeing the couple wanted to reduce the estate tax liability of their holding company, the advisor recommended a tax-free asset transfer.

The couple would sell their personal policy to their corporation. We had an actuary review their policy to determine the current market value of the policy. Based on their age and health, it was determined that the policy was worth approximately $250,000.

This meant that they would receive approximately $250,000 from their corporation by selling the policy to the company. When they pass away, the proceeds from the insurance policy would be received by the corporation and passed through the Capital Dividend Account (CDA) tax-free to their beneficiaries.

The couple incurred some personal taxes on the gain in value between the time they purchased the insurance policy to when they sold it to their company, but the tax liability was minimal, and the tax-free benefit was substantial.

These real life examples help illustrate the importance of integrated wealth management and working with a team of professionals, who consult together to understand your complete financial picture.

Why send the government money when you and your family can make much better use of it?

Good advisors can and will make a difference in your financial health and wealth.

Can you see how not doing so could have a negative effect on your financial resources?

Working with a financial advisor who is capable of delivering integrated wealth planning, who has access to a team of lawyers, accountants, financial planners, estate planners, business and farm succession specialists, or has strong relationships with outside team of professionals *is critical to your financial well-being.*

Taxation represents the single largest expense and loss of capital in the lives of many business and family farms, particularly in the retirement phase.

Financial advisors who can offer access to integrated wealth planning services can help affluent families, business owners, and farm families understand the complex tax and financial issues that they will face.

Doing so will minimize loss of business or farm wealth when important transitions or transactions occur.

The focus of wealth planning should be tax minimization, wealth planning, business or farm succession, and estate planning, including:

- Planning for the tax efficient transfer of the family business or farm to the next generation;
- Pre-retirement planning for the tax-efficient sale of the business or farm inventory and other assets;
- Planning tax efficient business or farm structures for the family business or farm and other ventures;
- Personal tax and estate planning;
- Financial and retirement planning.

Wealth Advisors should incorporate not only tax, estate, and financial planning, but also tax-efficient managed wealth solutions and insurance strategies, all personalized to meet the unique needs and values of each client family.

Integrated Investment and Wealth Management

What you pay a *Wealth Advisor* will depend on the level of services offered. The fee could be as low as 1.25% for pure investment advice to as high as 2.5% for integrated investment and wealth management advice.

These services should include:

1. Comprehensive Reporting;

2. A Personal Investment Plan;

3. True Global Portfolio Diversification;

4. Portfolio Diversification by Industry;

5. Portfolio Diversification by Investment Style: Growth, Value, and Alpha;

6. Portfolio diversification by *Asset Class*: Bonds, Stocks, *Real Estate* & *Private Equity*;

7. Portfolio Tax Deferral on Non-Registered Accounts;

8. Portfolio Downside Risk Management;

9. Regular Portfolio Rebalancing;

10. Dynamic Currency Hedging;

11. A Backing of a Professional Portfolio Management Team;

12. A Dedicated Investment Management Team Overseeing the Portfolio Managers;

13. Custom Portfolio Design;

14. Investment Fee Transparency;

15. A Financial Plan;

16. A Risk Management Plan;

17. A Personal Tax Plan;

18. A Business / Farm Tax Plan;

19. A Business / Farm Succession Plan;

20. An Estate Plan.

Integrated Wealth Management

Helping Your Family

Helping Children
Education
Gifting strategies
Business funding

Helping Parents
Long-term care
Managing estate
Care giving

Unexpected Demands
Emergency fund
Disability
Critical illness
Life insurance

Protecting Fa
Disability
Critical illness
Life insurance
Long-term ca

Enjoying Your Lifestyle

Home
Investing proceeds
Utilizing equity
Vacation home funding
Home insurance

Leisure & Travel
Remote banking access
Travel insurance
Emergency fund
Foreign tax rules

Work Options
Tax planning
Benefit plan
Income management

Protecting Lif
Disability/Crit
Life insurance
Cash flow pro

Anticipating the Future

Health Changes
Disability
Critical illness
Life insurance
Long-term care

New Opportunities
Investment funding
Short-term financing
Loans
Emergency funds

Business Succession
Business valuation
Tax planning
Investing proceeds
Financial purchase

Life on your (
Wealth mana
Portfolio eval
Cash flow an
Benefits and

Creating Financial Comfort

Managing Nest Egg
Asset allocation
Investment selection
Tax planning
Income options

Income planning
Tax planning
Income layering
RRSP conversion
Minimization strategies

Minimizing Taxes
Tax planning
Asset selection
Income layering
Tax-loss selling

Savings & Sp
Retirement fi
Systematic w
Systematic p

Leaving a Legacy

Wills & instructions
Estate plan
Tax planning
Trust services
Asset management

Charitable Giving
Planned giving strategy
Tax planning
Estate bequest

Living Legacy
Gifting family
Gifting community
Charitable giving

Maximizing Y
Universal & w
Segregated fu
Testamentan
Family trusts

Source Published with Permission: Barry LaValley, President, The Retirement Lifestyle Center

CHAPTER 13

CREATING MULTI-GENERATIONAL FAMILY WEALTH

Wealth Accumulation, Preservation, and Distribution

You have worked hard over the years to accumulate your wealth, and continue to work hard to grow it. Making these assets last for your lifetime and beyond is quite the challenge. A *Wealth Advisor* will help you preserve the wealth you've built and maximize growth without undue risk.

Since retirement is the beginning of a new phase of your life, which could last 20 – 30 years, your accumulated assets need to provide the desired lifestyle during retirement, keep pace with inflation, provide for increased health costs and ensure your legacy remains intact.

Wealth Advisors work collaboratively with a team of professionals alongside your professionals to discuss your lifestyle wishes in retirement, your desire to continue to build your estate, preserve and enhance what you have accumulated, maximize its tax efficiency and ensure that it passes intact to future generations while meeting your philanthropic objectives.

Wealth Advisors takes a holistic approach to managing your wealth that goes beyond simply managing your investments. *Wealth Advisors* will provide coordinated strategies that integrate investment management, portfolio construction, wealth planning, business or farm succession planning, estate planning, planned giving, and personalized advice. In short, they take a comprehensive, multi-disciplinary approach to managing your financial affairs.

Drawing on the expertise of their team of accounting, legal, financial, insurance, banking, business and farm succession planning, and estate planning professionals, *Wealth Advisors*, work closely with your legal and accounting team to provide you with a unique wealth advisory experience. Together, they would use their expertise and resources to provide you with greater financial flexibility.

Experienced *Wealth Advisors* have years of experience in dealing with the sophisticated needs of affluent clients. They are best positioned to deliver an individually structured wealth solution – one that reflects the complexities of your investment, wealth, and estate situation.

8 Steps to Creatng Multi-Generational Family Wealth

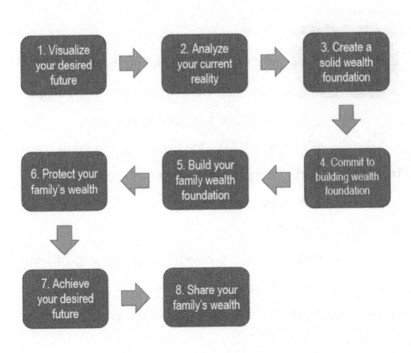

Step 1 - VISUALIZE – your family's desired future

1. Visualize your desired future

Your relationship with your *Wealth Advisor* begins with them having a conversation with you to help you visualize your desired future.

Wealth Advisors will take the time to get to know your true fears, challenges, advantages, excitements, opportunities, lifetime goals and aspirations for your family, legacy, and yourself.

Expect them to spend a considerable amount of time helping you visualize what your future could hold, and then create a summary report outlining the steps you should take to achieve it.

Step 2 - ANALYZE – your family's current reality

2. Analyze your current reality

Before your *Wealth Advisor* can begin the process of optimizing your wealth, they need to understand your current reality.

This involves exploring all the areas of your personal, family, and business life that have a financial impact on your wealth.

This results in a high-level projection of your net wealth and sufficiency of financial resources that will help you meet the objectives revealed in **step 1**

Step 3 - CREATE – a solid family wealth foundation

3. Create a solid wealth foundation

To create a solid family wealth foundation, you need to establish a solid investment foundation.

Before a *Wealth Advisor* can build your *Optimal Portfolio*, they need to design a blueprint of how your money will be managed.

They begin by creating a document called an *Investment Policy Statement* (**IPS**). This document captures what they learned about you in **Step 1** and **Step 2**.

The IPS summarizes your needs for:

- Income;

- Time horizon;

- Risk tolerance;

- Growth expectations;

- Liquidity requirements;

- Income tax characteristics;

- Anticipated changes in lifestyle;

- Economic variables, such as inflation and market volatility.

The **IPS** outlines the strategies the investment management team will employ to build your *Optimal Portfolio*. This provides a blueprint of how your discretionary *Portfolio Manager* will manage your investments.

Step 4 – COMMIT – to building your family wealth foundation

4. Commit to building wealth foundation

The next step is to hire a discretionary *Portfolio Manager* to build your *Optimal Portfolio*, as outlined in **Step 3**.

Your *Optimal Portfolio* is designed to maximize your investment growth while staying within your comfort zone in up markets as well as protect your capital in down markets.

This is achieved by combining different investment styles, *Asset Classes,* and exposure to various geographic regions and automatic rebalancing.

Tax efficiency is achieved using tax-advantaged investment structures and appropriate tax planning strategies to minimize overall family tax liability on your investments.

Step 5 - BUILD – your family's wealth foundation

5. Build your family wealth foundation

This is where I empower you to simplify your life and optimize your wealth so you can achieve your family's multi-generational goals of wealth accumulation, preservation, and distribution.

Drawing on the expertise of their team of accounting, legal, financial, insurance, banking, and estate planning professionals, *Wealth Advisors* work closely with your legal and accounting team to consolidate your sophisticated, complex financial reality.

They will analyze a variety of possible solutions, including wealth preservation and tax planning strategies across multiple generations, to protect and enhance your wealth.

Your *Wealth Advisor* will explore strategies and solutions that may help you to achieve your family's desired future. The outcome—a legacy of significance for your family and cherished causes.

Step 6 - PROTECT – your family's wealth

6. Protect your family's wealth

What's the point of working hard to grow your family wealth if you do nothing to protect it.

Your *Wealth Advisor* will identify and manage the financial risks that may prevent you from achieving your multi-generational goals of wealth accumulation, preservation, and distribution.

Your *Wealth Advisor* will review work collaboratively with their insurance experts to implement all effective insurance and estate planning strategies that will assist you in achieving your personal and business goals.

Some of these strategies include:

- Protecting your family and business;

- Tax-sheltering investments;

- Supplementary retirement income;

- Planning your business succession;

- Offsetting estate taxes to keep assets intact.

Step 7 - ACHIEVE – your family's desired future

7. Achieve your desired future

The implementation process is sometimes lengthy as the material is intense. It takes time to decide on the most efficient course of action for you to follow.

Your *Wealth Advisor* should meet with you every six to twelve months, or more often, if necessary, to implement and monitor your progress.

They should also document any major changes in your personal or financial situation that require them to adjust your multi-generational family wealth plan.

Step 8 - SHARE – your family's wealth

> ### 8. Share your family's wealth

This step is the culmination of implementing your family multi-generational wealth plan.

You have optimized your wealth, achieved your lifetime goals and aspirations, and put in place a multi-generational legacy for your family and cherished causes.

However, your **Wealth Advisor's** work is not done.

Your **Wealth Advisor** should continue to meet with you, and eventually, your heirs every six to twelve months or more often if necessary, to ensure your estate plan and legacy remains on track.

CHAPTER 14

CONCLUSION

As you can see, if you have gone through this information in detail, managing your financial assets is much more than handing off the decision-making to a financial advisor (stockbroker, mutual fund salesman, insurance salesman, or The Nice Lady at the Bank).

It involves understanding all types of financial advisors and which services they offer.

It also means understanding how they are paid for their services (no one works for free).

It also means that you get what you pay for.

Better services will generally cost more initially, but good advice will save you money, taxes, and headaches.

The wealth you accumulated over the years will be professionally managed and provide for your family and charitable interests.

DOWNLOAD MY FREE BOOKS

Planning to Sell your Business or transfer it to the next generation? Please check out my new book:

Ready to Sell Your Business?

or Transfer it to The Next Generation

To get your free book visit:

www.readytosellyourbusiness.com

Planning to Sell your Farm or transfer it to the next generation? *Please check out my new book:*

Ready to Sell Your Farm?

or Transfer it to The Next Generation

To get your free book visit:

www.readytosellyourfarm.com

Planning to Sell your farm or transfer it to the next generation? Please check out my new book:

How to Sell Your Farm Successfully

or Transfer it to The Next Generation

To get your free book visit:

www.howtosellyourfarm.com

Made in the USA
Middletown, DE
24 January 2021